# *So You Want to Work on a Boat*

## Thor Robert Erikson

ISBN-10: 1475059388
ISBN-13: 978-1475059380

## DEDICATION

This book is dedicated to mariners who serve on
commercial vessels throughout the world. These
hardworking women and men make an immeasurably
valuable contribution to society. Yet they work in jobs that
many people know little about, in terms of the special skills
required, the unique hazards faced, and the difficult
sacrifices made.

# CONTENTS

So You Want to Work on a Boat

**Commercial mariners are often** responsible for the safety and well-being of large numbers of passengers. As such, the industry imposes high levels of accountability, whether the work setting is an inland tour vessel or a transatlantic ocean liner. This may explain the strict standards, in terms of licensing, inspection, and safety regulations. The *Queen Mary 2*, pictured below, is owned by Cunard Line, which also operates the *Queen Elizabeth* and *Queen Victoria*. Job opportunities that arise on passenger vessels of this size cover a broad range of departments, including deck, engine, security, environmental, entertainment, culinary, housekeeping, and casino, among others.

**I'm not working down here!** In the early 1900s, perhaps the best way to describe the machinery spaces of large ships was as an infernal hell... unbearable heat, deafening noise, airborne cinders, and coal dust from bunkers. In the photo above, stokers rake burning cinders from a boiler on the *USS Leviathan* in 1919. Originally built as the *SS Vaterland* for Hamburg America Line, the *Leviathan* served as a troop transport during World War I. After the war, it entered service with United States Lines. In the photo below, it steams out of New York Harbor in July 1934. Mercifully, the job of stoker in such harsh settings no longer exists. This book covers the many jobs that are available for commercial mariners today, and how to go about getting those jobs.

# *Introduction*

Yes sir, I want to work on a boat! That's the life for me. I don't want to be part of that nine-to-five rat race. I want to do something meaningful with my life, like piloting a steel vessel. I want to be in the wheelhouse of a tugboat and feel a sense of pride in my navigation skills. I want to wear a crisp white uniform as a purser on a cruise ship and be part of an important team.

I want to put on a hard hat and work in the engine room of a container ship, climbing to the top of a giant diesel engine to inspect fuel injectors. I want to be a deckhand on a commuter ferry where passengers smile at me every morning because they know I look out for their safety. I want to learn how to splice wire rope. I want to learn how to use radar. I want to learn how to troubleshoot refrigeration systems. I want to learn how to read navigational charts. I want to work on a boat!

Working on the water can seem like a unique lifestyle, appealing to the rugged individualist in everyone. It can seem like an unexplored jewel of a job market, far from the crowds that desperately line up to work in offices and factories. After all, we hear stories of people coming home with fat wallets after working a few months on commercial fishing boats. We hear of entry-level deckhands becoming captains in a few short years on offshore supply vessels. We hear of oil tanker crews who support their families working six months a year.

While such stories can hold true, the industry is neither undiscovered nor unexplored. Like other sectors of the labor market in this difficult economy, many have tread where eager newcomers take their first steps. That doesn't mean job opportunities aren't out there. But not every job opportunity is the same, and not everyone walks away with the same measure of personal and financial satisfaction.

**Who makes the most money in this industry?** Some of the highest salaries on the water are earned by marine pilots, who can make over $200,000 a year. A marine pilot provides guidance to vessels as they transit unfamiliar stretches of water. Deck officers rely on a pilot's knowledge of local currents, reefs, sunken wrecks, and other obstructions. Pilots also assist in docking operations. It's a job that requires tremendous experience in handling large vessels. Soon after stepping aboard an unfamiliar 60,000 ton bulk carrier, a pilot must assess how the ship will respond to engine and rudder commands. There is little time for familiarization with a ship's maneuvering peculiarities and navigation electronics. Pilot candidates generally need several years of experience on an unlimited master license to even be considered by a pilot board. In addition to requiring great skill, the job is dangerous. Pilots board large vessels at all hours, day or night, in almost all sea conditions.

If one thing is certain in this industry, it's this. Jobs on commercial vessels involve hard work and offer some very genuine occupational hazards. Why then would anyone want to do it? Working for a living is difficult enough without throwing in the added possibility of being able to drown on the job.

It isn't easy being a deckhand on a New England passenger ferry when wind and rain cut across your face on a cold February morning. There's nothing enjoyable about being a tankerman on an ammonia barge in the middle of August on the Mississippi River. Yet, there are long lines to get these jobs. People have different reasons for gravitating toward this line of work.

One of the major draws for working on the water is that salaries can be attractive. The maritime industry and merchant marine have traditionally been known for high paying jobs. However, high salaries are not a universal attribute of working on the water. There are many entry-level positions that offer entry-level salaries.

Additionally, some entry-level positions have high turnover rates, when new hires develop second thoughts about the difficult or dangerous working conditions they're getting themselves into for $9 or $10 an hour. Higher salaries are commanded when commercial mariners acquire Coast Guard licenses, endorsements, hands-on experience... and the good fortune of being hired by a reputable company.

Some people are drawn to the industry because they want to sock away money. When you work on a boat for the long haul, the boat is home. Meals are provided by the company. Berthing is provided by the company. There aren't too many places to spend money on an oil rig in the Shetland Islands or a tanker carrying bulk chemicals to South America.

And since a person is captive on a vessel, there's an incentive to work overtime when opportunities arise. For commuter ferries, this issue might be irrelevant, since crews often go home after getting off watch. But on coastal or offshore vessels, working at sea could provide the opportunity to save money for a car or downpayment on a house.

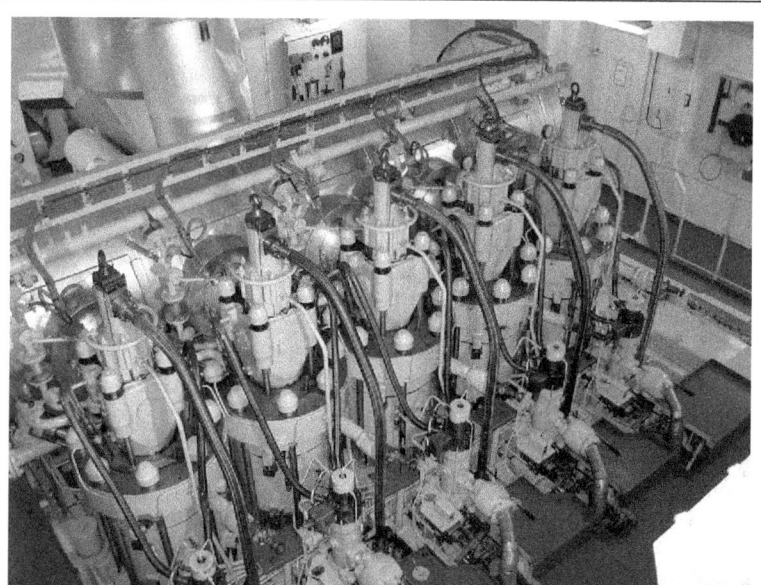

**This MAN B&W 5S50MC 5-cylinder 2-stroke cycle engine** is representative of low-speed marine diesels used on medium-sized cargo ships today. Wipers, QMEDs, and engineering officers (whose jobs are described in the chapters ahead) ensure that such engines operate with a proper supply of cooling water, lubricating oil, and diesel fuel. There's lots of preventive maintenance involved in keeping such an expensive piece of machinery running for the life of a vessel. This includes regular analysis of lube oil, as well as diligent inspection of cylinders, connecting rods, crossheads, and turbochargers. The photo above shows fuel injectors on top of the cylinder heads, but there's a massive engine block that's two stories tall underneath those deck plates.

But it's not only about salary and socking away money. Serving on commercial vessels can appeal to some people because the nature of work is unique. There isn't any land-based equivalent of working as a deckhand aboard a towboat on the Ohio River. Nor is there a land-based equivalent of serving as second officer on a cruise ship.

The deckhand can take pride in handling lines, assembling large tows, and maintaining safety equipment in compliance with Coast Guard regulations. On a cruise ship, the second officer is in charge of navigation. She may take pride in testing junior officers and ratings on their celestial navigation and chart reading skills. An engineer on an offshore supply vessel may take immense satisfaction in being able to tell something is wrong with his engines the instant he steps aboard. Many commercial mariners carry a deep sense of pride about the work they do.

Some people like the unconventional schedules, involving long stretches of work followed by generous time off. Someone who works on a crude oil tanker making runs to the Persian Gulf might work three straight months, after which she has an entire month off. Someone who works on a towboat may work 28 days on, and then be off for 14 days.

For some people, those large windows of personal time can provide opportunities to pursue hobbies, tackle large home improvement projects, or take unconventional vacations. However, not everyone sees this aspect of working on boats as a boon. Some people would rather be with their families on a daily basis, coming home for dinner at night and going to work the next morning, instead of being thrust upon their loved ones for two straight weeks.

Some people are drawn to working on the water because of the chance to travel. Working on commercial vessels can offer opportunities to see places that most folks would pay lots of money to see. Naturally, this depends on the type of vessel. If you sign up for a berth on a container ship making runs between Seattle and the Far East, your itinerary is rather fixed.

**Ocean or inland?** A major decision for commercial mariners is whether to seek employment on ocean-going, offshore, coastal, or inland vessels, with salary being a major consideration. But it isn't always easy to correlate bigger vessels and deeper waters with higher salaries. It can depend on an employer. Quality of life issues enter the equation too, so that one might be willing to make a little less, but work 20 straight days instead of 60 straight days.

Given the efficiency of modern container terminals in loading cargo, port stays are measured in terms of 36 or 48 hours instead of seven or ten days. Gone are the days where ships linger for a week in exotic North African ports while crews visit street fairs and archeological ruins. It isn't like the 1930s, where life in the merchant marine is some romantic and adventurous way to see the world from a tramp steamer.

The maritime industry today is highly automated and highly efficient. Aside from that, many cargo terminals are situated in non-residential areas where crewmembers might not want to venture far from their ship at night. There are boats which are geared around fun destinations. For instance, yacht crews could get to see Caribbean ports and the French Riviera. Cruise ships venture into every sea on the face of the earth, from the Southern Ocean to the Mediterranean, offering crews a chance to see everything from polar bears on ice floes to coral reefs in clear azure waters.

**Seasonal job markets,** such as ferry operations, can require early planning. Some ferry systems start hiring in the early spring for their summer workforce, especially in northern latitudes. *Yakima* is owned by Washington State Ferries, which operates the largest ferry fleet in the United States. The diesel-electric ferry is 382 feet long and 73 feet wide, with a draft of 18 feet 6 inches. Weighing in at 2,704 tons, *Yakima* can carry 2,000 passengers and 144 vehicles. Its four engines produce 8,000 horsepower, providing a speed of 17 knots. 1 Washington State Ferries serves Puget Sound and its surrounding waters, carrying commuters and tourists.

But it's important to remember that cruise ship and yacht crews work very hard when they're at sea. Yacht crews put in long hours to provide extraordinary levels of service for guests who might be paying $15,000 a week for a charter. Cruise ship dining room personnel run themselves ragged providing an endless conveyor belt of meals, buffet tables, and snacks for ravenous passengers. This means sightseeing is something that's done when you're free for the day and not burned out from working twelve straight days in a row.

There are definitely benefits to working on a boat. But there are drawbacks as well. Working on a boat is, for better or worse, a state of confinement. For thirty days, your world could be 85 feet in length and 25 feet in width. That can mean not going out with friends on Friday nights. It can mean the end of lunch breaks on a park bench. It can mean missing little league soccer games and pizza nights with kids.

Thanks to modern technology, the element of isolation from loved ones isn't as bad as it used to be. Well-appointed commercial vessels usually have internet access, satellite phones, e-mail, and other features to make life on the water more pleasant. Vessel operators who invest in such amenities enjoy dividends in terms of better crew morale. However, there is no escaping the hardship of physically being apart from loved ones and friends.

In addition to the confinement and isolation, working on a boat introduces stress in the form of a reduced level of privacy. If you're considering an entry-level position on a commercial vessel, forget about the notion of privacy. Whether you're a deckhand on a fishing boat or an audio technician on a cruise ship, there's no such thing as private cabins.

Unless you're a captain or an officer, you'll share a cabin with one, two, or maybe three bunkmates. For some, this aspect of work can be seen as something that comes with the territory. For a young person, it might even seem like fun. But for a middle-aged person accustomed to sharing a bedroom with only a spouse, it can take some personal adjustment, which isn't necessarily pleasant.

Another thing about working on boats is that schedules can be demanding. Unlike conventional nine-to-five jobs, many boat jobs involve standing watches. A watch is a shift where someone works a fixed post position for four, five, six, or seven hours. Some mariners can find themselves working twelve hours straight due to a lack of relief personnel.

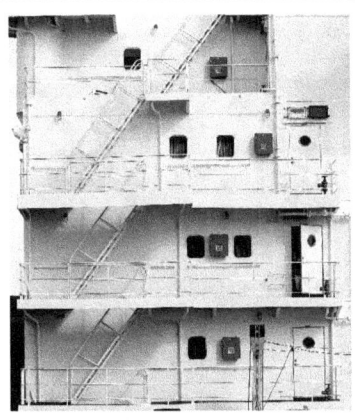

**Do I get my own private cabin?** That can depend on the type of vessel. Junior personnel on small and medium-sized commercial vessels generally share cabins. Officers on large ocean-going vessels usually get private cabins. On a cruise ship with a crew roster of 900 people, three or four to a cabin for non-officers is typical. On a 1,000' tanker with a crew of 22, living space is plentiful and accommodations are usually very generous for everyone.

Fixed post doesn't necessarily mean being confined to a single location. It can, in the case of a mate in the wheelhouse of a tugboat, but it essentially means being confined to watchstanding duties. For a deckhand, that can mean being sent forward on a barge to serve as a lookout. It can mean breaking out portable running lights from the equipment locker, or going down to the engine room to hold a bracket for the chief to weld.

Watchstanding is standard fare in the military, but in the civilian sector, standing watches can require adjustments in lifestyle for the uninitiated. For someone coming from the Navy watch system of six on, six off, it can be just another day at the office. For an ex-submariner, it could even seem restful not to wolf down lunch in 15 minutes to make room for the next meal seating.

But for someone coming from a nine-to-five customer service job in a warehouse, it could be a real bear to get off watch, try to squeeze in five hours of sleep, and then do it over and over again… when there's no refuge from the drone of a diesel engine, footsteps in passageways, doors opening and closing throughout the boat, and light seeping in through portholes.

**Is specialized education necessary for working on commercial vessels?** It depends on a person's ambitions. There are numerous entry-level positions for which specialized training and education, other than a basic STCW course, are not mandatory. But if someone is serious about career advancement, the answer is yes. Standing watches as a deck officer on the bridge of a vessel like the one pictured above requires knowledge in a number of areas. These include celestial navigation, electronic navigation, collision regulations, and other complex subjects. Training and education are offered through maritime academies, specialized colleges, private institutions, and self-study programs. This subject is covered in greater detail in Chapter 7, *Training and Education*. But the bottom line is that training and education are necessary investments for attaining desirable high-level positions.

Working on the water can also present unique occupational hazards. While a bookkeeper at a construction company doesn't worry about the possibility of being swept overboard during the workday, a crab fisherman on the Bering Sea does. There are other risks as well. Commercial mariners work on decks that are at times awash in seawater or coated with ice.

**The merchant marine officer license** Qualified candidates can sit for license exams after satisfying sea time requirements. Deck license subjects include navigation, seamanship, collision regulations, cargo operations, ship construction, meteorology, and related subjects. Engine license subjects include diesels, boilers, steam turbines, gas turbines, auxiliaries, electricity, refrigeration, and related subjects. License exams cover a wide range of tonnages, horsepower ratings, endorsements, and geographical limitations. Each exam is specific to the grade of license and endorsement sought. See Chapter 6 for sample license questions. Above is an old version of a license. The new version resembles a passport booklet.

It's easy to fall and sustain injuries in such settings. This is especially true when a vessel is rolling or pitching in severe sea conditions. These risks are intensified on fishing vessels, where pot haulers and other gear can swing around at the level of a person's head. Employment on inland rivers can spare one from working in ten foot seas, but that doesn't mean conditions are easy.

**Tough legal standards** The bulk carrier *Selendang Ayu* lost power and foundered off Unalaska Island in December 2004, releasing 340,000 gallons of oil. 2 In prosecuting the matter, the U.S. Department of Justice argued that the engine failure was attributable to improper maintenance. Such legal issues are discussed in Chapter 8, *Commercial Mariners and Maritime Law.*

A deckhand on an inland towboat can work all day under the hot sun, lashing together barges for a tow, or breaking apart tows to fit through canal locks. In that type of work, a single misstep could mean falling into the water between two barges, with fatal consequences. On boats of all sizes, engine room personnel are exposed to high noise levels. If proper precautions aren't taken, such conditions could lead to permanent hearing loss.

On vessels carrying solvents and chemicals, crews can be exposed to toxic fumes. Such hazards can be intensified when entering confined spaces for inspections or repairs. Working on boats can require lifting heavy objects, such as intake manifolds or electric motors, and carrying them up narrow and steep stairways or ladders.

As if all that isn't enough, let's add the fact that this is a highly regulated industry. Commercial mariners must comply with extensive credentialing requirements to qualify for many seagoing positions. This can mean getting a MMC, or Merchant Mariner Credential. It can mean obtaining STCW certification, which comes from the

International Convention on Standards of Training, Certification and Watchkeeping for Seafarers. Then there's the TWIC, or Transportation Worker Identification Credential. All these things cost money and time to obtain.

**Working on a commercial vessel is not for everyone.** Some readers may decide that this line of work really isn't for them... in terms of credentialing requirements, quality of life issues, or watchstanding routines. For those who want to work in the maritime industry without being in the service of a vessel, there are other options. These include insurance, surveying, shipbuilding, and sales, to name a few. Naturally, these fields have their own educational requirements, ranging from a high school diploma to an advanced degree. An insurance claim representative handles claims for cargo damage, hull & machinery damage, or personal injury. Marine claims can be large and complex. In July 2006, the Mitsui OSK car carrier *Cougar Ace* was en route from Japan to the United States with a cargo of 4,703 new Mazdas. When the ship approached U.S. waters, something went wrong during ballasting operations. As a result, the ship took on a severe list, causing cargo to shift. Because of concerns over how this affected the cars, Mazda destroyed them. 3 Although they don't always handle $40 million automobile claims like this one, claim representatives handle a variety of other types of losses, such as paper rolls damaged by saltwater or steel coils damaged by rust.

For higher-level mariners who pursue licenses, there's the cost of prep courses, along with the task of verifying sea time. Physical exams are another barrier for some, where even long-time veterans in the industry can face difficulties in license renewal because of medical conditions.

---

**"Stronger measures were necessary.** As soon as Quartermaster Rowe reached the bridge, Captain Smith asked if he had brought the rockets. Rowe produced them, and the Captain ordered, 'Fire one, and fire one every five or six minutes.' " 4 "Second Officer Herbert Stone, pacing the *Californian's* bridge, also kept his eye on this strange steamer. At 12:45 he saw a sudden flash of white light burst over her. Strange, he thought, that a ship would fire rockets at night." 5 "Second-class passenger Lawrence Beesley considered himself the rankest landlubber, but even he knew what rockets meant. The *Titanic* needed help - needed it so badly she was calling on any ship near enough to see." 6

*Question 1:* Which of the following conditions represents the appropriate time for setting off distress flares and rockets? (a.) only when there is a chance of them being seen by rescue vessels (b.) at half-hour intervals (c.) at one hour intervals (d.) immediately upon abandoning vessel    Answer below

---

*Thomas Andrews:* The pumps buy you time, but minutes only. From this moment, no matter what we do, *Titanic* will founder.
*Ismay:* But this ship can't sink!
*Thomas Andrews:* She's made of iron, sir! I assure you, she can... and she will. It is a mathematical certainty.
*Smith:* How much time?
*Thomas Andrews:* An hour... two at most. 7

*Question 2:* Flooding of any compartment in a ship, resulting in a serious loss of reserve buoyancy, will always _____. (a.) increase ship stability (b.) reduce ship stability (c.) cause a serious permanent list (d.) decrease the heeling moment    Answer below

These are questions of the type that have appeared in license exams. They are not endorsed by the U.S. Coast Guard as license exam questions. Additional sample questions appear in Chapter 6.    Answers: 1(a)   2(b) 8

---

On the surface, the industry could be seen as exciting and free-spirited. Yes, there is the thrill of seeing new places, meeting new people, and acquiring new skills. One can feel a sense of exhilaration in passing a license exam or learning how to plot a course.

**The government sector** offers ocean, coastal, and inland opportunities with good salaries and benefits. Government employers include the U.S. Military Sealift Command, National Oceanic and Atmospheric Administration, and U.S. Army Corps of Engineers. Positions in this sector include mates, engineers, oilers, deckhands, fishermen, and cooks, among others. There are also opportunities within municipal agencies dealing with fisheries, conservation, environmental protection, and wastewater treatment. Pictured above, the Army Corps of Engineers towboat *City of Ottawa* is only 76 feet in length, but it turns two stainless steel propellers measuring almost six and a half feet in diameter (76"). Powered by twin 1,050 horsepower Caterpillar diesels, the 12 knot vessel has accommodations for 5 crew. ₉ The Army Corps of Engineers handles a wide range of services that includes dredging, lock operation, and coastal protection. This is discussed in greater detail in the chapter ahead.

But for the most part, the routine is strict. Shipboard life is more regimented than working in a factory or office. Getting sick as a commercial mariner could mean that the person on watch you were scheduled to relieve now has to put in a twelve-hour shift. The level of accountability is also demanding. A minor collision or grounding could cause millions of dollars worth of environmental damage to a delicate ecosystem. It could result in the lay-up of a vessel in a shipyard for weeks, where it won't be generating revenues for its owners.

A commercial vessel is expected to carry out a certain mission, such as carrying passengers or cargo from point A to point B within a given time period, and within a given budget for crew wages, fuel, supplies, and food. If it encounters delays, there can be penalties from cargo interests. If storms are encountered, injured passengers could sue. Although it might appear straightforward and mundane, the operation of a commercial vessel can be stressful.

To outsiders, the industry could seem like a laid back world where a mate could skip a few haircuts, grow a beard, and wear flip-flops to pick up a plate of scrambled eggs in galley. But despite the absence of strict dress codes or grooming standards on many vessels, life on a commercial vessel is one of tight conformity to established shipboard routines.

When a company puts a crew on the water, it expects a high degree of self-reliance from them. If there's a cargo fire at 3:00 a.m., the company expects that the crew will be able to deal with it. If the vessel experiences engine problems, the company feels confident that the captain won't enter into a financially unsound salvage agreement without exploring all other options. If a mate suffers a heart attack at the dinner table, the home office expects the crew to execute the company's emergency operating procedures. Commercial mariners have high levels of accountability to live up to.

This book isn't written with the intent of encouraging readers to seek employment on commercial vessels. Nor is it written to discourage anyone. It merely attempts to present information about the industry so that people who are interested in this line of work can learn more about fulfilling their ambitions. However, it should come as no surprise that the industry is not for everyone.

And for those who decide that working on a boat is not for them, there are many jobs in which they can be part of the maritime community without becoming a commercial mariner. These jobs are covered in greater detail in the last chapter, which should provide guidance for those who are inexplicably drawn to being around commercial vessels, but who feel that a berth aboard one doesn't quite fit their lifestyle.

Well, if you're still interested, read on. There's lots of material to cover. And good luck!

# *Where Are the Jobs?*

If you've ever looked for a job on an employment website such as *monster.com* or *careerbuilder.com*, you know the drill. You enter your search keywords and zip code, then select a distance you're willing to travel to work. You select 10 miles and come up with three leads. You select 20 miles and come up with eight leads, and so on.

It goes without say that the farther out on the horizon you look, the more opportunities you find. Everyone knows this. The interesting thing about working on the water is that commuting distance can become less important than with land-based employment. If a job involves working four weeks on and two weeks off, it might matter less whether an employer is 50 miles away or 5 miles away. This isn't to say it doesn't matter at all. But you're not driving that distance every day of the week. Many jobs on the water are mini-relocations of sorts. Commuting can be something akin to leaving your car in the airport long-term parking lot for a few weeks.

Why is this relevant? A big part of finding a job is being willing to get to where the job is. Naturally, there are more fundamental issues, such as one's skills and experience. But for a motivated jobseeker willing to make the effort to be in the right place at the right time, there are good job opportunities on the East Coast, West Coast and just about every nook and cranny in between.

It's also true that there are many qualified candidates going for those same good opportunities. And in the end, everyone doesn't necessarily walk away with a prize in their hand.

**An industry of ever-increasing efficiency** People might think of cargo operations as a labor-intensive process where pallets of goods are hoisted out of ships' holds using traditional block and tackle gear. This was the common means of unloading vessels in the past. While some types of cargo are still handled that way, containerization has revolutionized the industry. For commercial mariners, this has translated into shorter port stays. *Osaka Express* is a good example of a modern container ship. Owned and operated by Hapag-Lloyd, one of the world's largest container lines, the 103,662 ton (DWT) ship is 1099 feet long and 138 feet wide. Its container capacity is 8,749 TEU. Containers typically come in 20 foot, 40 foot, and 55 foot lengths, with ships being rated by the number of 20 foot containers they can carry. The acronym TEU stands for twenty-foot equivalent unit. A 46,230 horsepower plant gives *Osaka Express* a speed of 20 knots, which is adequate for global shipping. Built in 2007, it is a young ship by any standards. 10

But applicants who are qualified, tenacious, and who have reasonable expectations do succeed more often than not. Sometimes people take positions for which they're overqualified, hoping that someone might retire or leave to create the vacancy they really want.

For instance, if a 200 ton mate doesn't find what he's looking for in the wheelhouse, many companies wouldn't turn him away if he expressed interest in working as senior deckhand. Not surprisingly, this type of job placement can make competition stiffer on the lower rungs of the food chain. But it is a reality in today's economy.

Jobs on commercial vessels might be seen as one big employment pool. That's kind of the way the U.S. Department of Labor treats the industry. In its statistics for job growth and other indexes, the federal government essentially designates jobs on the water as marine transportation jobs.

But there are many different sectors under this very broad heading. In the inland and coastal employment market, there are jobs on tugboats, offshore supply vessels, mobile offshore drilling units, dive support vessels, commercial fishing vessels, ferries, dinner cruise boats, and tour boats. In the ocean market, there are container ships, tankers, cruise ships, bulk carriers, and research vessels. There are jobs on yachts, which are private vessels in most instances.

Every industry is different, and at any given time, subject to the winds of change that affect its fortunes. The drilling moratorium imposed in the wake of the *Deepwater Horizon* explosion seriously affected job opportunities on offshore supply vessels and tugs in the Gulf of Mexico. The tightening of corporate purse strings for executive outings continues to affect dinner cruise markets nationwide.

The growth of the aquaculture industry has impacted a number of important fisheries, such as Alaskan salmon. International steel prices affect production in the Midwest, which in turn sets the stage for job prospects aboard ore carriers on the Great Lakes. Like shifting sands on the desert, job markets in any given sector can change overnight.

**What exactly is a tug?** We all know that the word "tug" identifies a hardworking boat that carries out many different duties. It's funny that the word can define such a wide array of vessels. The Log Bronc tugs pictured above fit the bill in that they are powered by diesel engines and robustly constructed of steel. Although such tugs earn their keep working in tough settings, they're compact enough to be transported on tractor trailer trucks. Interestingly enough, the word "tug" can also identify a 2,528 ton anchor handling vessel, such as the *Viking Troll*, pictured on the opposite page.

But this book isn't about forecasting and analyzing business trends in the maritime industry. It's about working on commercial vessels. So let's get down to business and start covering the places where people can find work. The following pages list the various types of vessels on which job opportunities regularly arise.

**Tugboats and Towboats** In terms of the number of companies that operate tugboats and towboats, this is a very large sector of the commercial vessel industry. Some operators specialize in towing, while others handle ship assist, ship escort, salvage, and other services. Some of the major companies here include Crowley Maritime

Corporation, Foss Maritime Corporation, Moran Towing Corporation, and McAllister Towing & Transportation. A list of tugboat companies is provided at the end of the book.

**A 25' steel workboat** could be called a tug by its operators. The word "tug" could also identify a vessel that operates in all the cold, stormy, and inhospitable corners of the Arctic Ocean or North Sea. The *Viking Troll*, pictured above, serves the energy industry by performing anchor handling operations and carrying supplies. With a length exceeding 242 feet and a 25-foot summer draft, it is by no means your typical harbor tug. Although its main engines produce 15,000 horsepower, the combined output of its three 816 horsepower thrusters alone exceeds the total power of many inland tugs. 11

**Oil & Gas Industry Vessels** These vessels support the oil, gas, and energy exploration industries. In the United States, these jobs are predominantly found in the Gulf of Mexico. Positions arise on crew boats, offshore supply vessels, exploration vessels, and other utility vessels. Crew boats are high-speed vessels that shuttle crews to and from oil rigs.

There are also jobs on MODUs, or mobile offshore drilling units. These can be of the semi-submersible or jack-up type. In addition to positions arising on these specialized craft, there are other oil and energy industry jobs, such as drilling supervisors, roughnecks, roustabouts, and commercial divers. Although this book doesn't cover those positions, there is a close interlocking relationship between commercial mariners and offshore oil platform workers. Businesses that operate these support vessels are included in the list of tugboat companies at the end of the book.

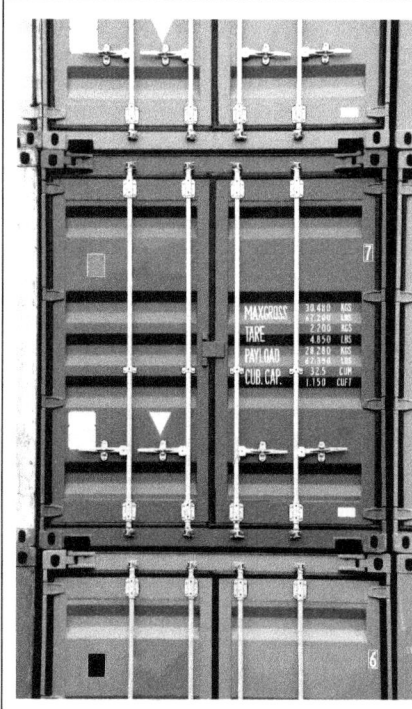

**A special job for seamen on container ships** From a distance, a container ship seems like the embodiment of simplicity in cargo transport. But closer examination reveals an intricate system of safeguards to keep all those neat stacks of "boxes" from toppling over. Twist-lock devices secure containers to one another. Notice the reinforced corners of each container, designed for this purpose. Additionally, lashing gear is used to fasten containers to one another. This consists of steel rods with turnbuckles. Rods are rigged from one container to another, after which turnbuckles are tightened. Setting up this gear is a physically demanding job that requires being comfortable with heights.

**Ocean-Going Cargo Vessels** This includes container ships, tankers, RO/RO ships, bulk carriers, and other cargo vessels. In the United States, large seagoing vessels also operate on the Great Lakes, carrying iron ore to steel production facilities. This is truly a global marketplace because ships are essentially international entities. They can be crewed by personnel from all over the world.

A vessel operator might have its corporate headquarters in a major city, but its ships could be registered under the flags of sovereign states in remote corners of the world. Some of the major cargo carriers include APL, Hapag-Lloyd, Maersk, and Overseas Shipping Group. See the list at the end of the book for additional carriers.

**Cruise Ships** This is one of the largest sectors of the maritime labor market. Similar to cargo ships, cruise ship employees come from every corner of the globe. This area has seen tremendous growth in recent decades. Judging from the number of 100,000-plus-ton cruise ships being built in shipyards around the world, the industry doesn't exhibit signs of slowing down anytime soon.

Cruise ships are interesting because they cover the broadest spectrum of jobs found on any commercial vessel. A large cargo ship will typically employ anywhere from fifteen to thirty crewmembers, composed of deck, engine, and steward's department personnel. In contrast, a large cruise ship can easily employ more than a thousand people, with positions in the culinary, housekeeping, security, medical, entertainment, purser, youth activities, casino, gift shop, and other departments... in addition to traditional deck and engine personnel.

The cruise industry can offer a way to see wonderful parts of the world while earning a paycheck. However, work schedules on cruise ships can be very demanding. Dining room, bar, culinary, housekeeping, and laundry personnel put in long hours. Depending on a cruise line, they might work every day for the time a ship is at sea, without a day off until docking. Some cruise ship positions involve working for contractors of a cruise line, such as a gift shop. Opening a gift shop at 10:00 a.m. and closing up at 10:00 p.m. while the ship is at sea can mean twelve-hour days for a shop manager.

Some positions on cruise ships offer base pay, with the remainder of compensation provided by passenger tips. Shipboard labor and pay policies are beyond the scope of this book. However, it's important to realize that cruise ships are not subject to a country's minimum wage laws just because they maintain corporate offices in that country.

**One of the less-explored job markets** Research vessels are a worthwhile avenue to investigate for both deck and engine applicants. With many jobseekers setting sights on tugboats, ferries, cruise ships, and cargo carriers, this area is sometimes overlooked. These vessels are recognized for their important oceanographic studies, but it's the deck and engine personnel that get the scientists to the Mariana Trench to do their research. The research vessel *Hi'ialakai* is operated by the National Oceanic and Atmospheric Administration. It works in the Hawaiian Islands and other parts of the Pacific that include American Samoa and the Mariana Islands. *Hi'ialakai's* research covers coral reef ecosystem mapping, coral reef health studies, bio-analysis assessments, and studies of fish stocks. This compact ship is 224 feet in length and has a displacement of 2,285 tons. It steams at 11 knots and has an impressive range of 8,000 nautical miles. 12

Many cruise ships are registered under the flags of The Bahamas, Panama, and other sovereign states. Therefore, someone in a large developed country might be surprised to learn that familiar labor laws are not necessarily applicable aboard many cruise ships. But this is true with other large ships and yachts as well.

Some of the well-known employers in this area include Carnival Cruise Line, Celebrity Cruises, Cunard Cruise Line, Disney Cruise Line, Holland America Line, Norwegian Cruise Line, and Royal Caribbean International. A list of cruise lines is provided at the end of the book.

**Research Vessels** conduct oceanographic, biological, meteorological, environmental, and other scientific research. They are operated by government and private sector employers. NOAA, or the National Oceanic and Atmospheric Administration, runs the largest fleet of research vessels in the United States. Its job postings appear on www.usajobs.gov, the federal employment website.

In addition to scientific research, NOAA acts as an enforcement agency through its National Marine Fisheries Services branch. It protects fish stocks from being overharvested by enforcing regulations for catch sizes, catch tonnages, and fishing seasons. Private sector research vessel operators include Woods Hole Oceanographic Institution, Scripps Institution of Oceanography, and Skidaway Institute of Oceanography. Private research vessels can be funded through universities, grants, and donations. A list of research vessel operators is provided at the end of the book.

**The U.S. Military Sealift Command** employs over 5,500 civilian mariners and operates about 110 non-combatant ships. It plays a number of vital roles in supporting the armed forces. These include replenishing naval ships, conducting specialized missions, prepositioning combat cargo around the world, and transporting equipment and supplies used by the armed forces of the United States and its allies. Its ships are jointly crewed by Navy and civilian mariners.

Perhaps one of the Military Sealift Command's most widely recognized roles is that of the Combat Logistics Force, made up of around 32 ships that provide underway replenishment to warships and support vessels. This involves the impressive feat of transferring fuel and supplies between two ships steaming at 13 or 14 knots. These vessels are crewed by civil service mariners, with some having a contingent of Navy personnel on board for support, coordination, and helicopter operations.

The Combat Logistics Force consists of fleet replenishment oilers, ammunition ships, fast combat support ships, and dry cargo-ammunition ships. Other vessels operated by MSC include prepositioning ships, hospital ships, tugboats, special mission ships, and vessels used in carrying out oceanographic and hydrographic surveys, underwater surveillance, missile tracking, acoustic surveys, and submarine & special warfare support. [13]

**Training Ships** This is a narrow slice of the job market. But it can be rewarding for people who enjoy sharing their knowledge with students who are training to become officers at the nation's maritime schools. When a training ship goes to sea, select faculty members supervise shipboard operations and teach classes. The schools sometimes hire personnel from the outside to assist in these areas. The stints are usually two or three months long.

The **U.S. Army Corps of Engineers** is a large government employer of commercial mariners. They provide engineering and construction services for military and civilian projects, many of which take place on coastal and inland waters. They oversee the operation and maintenance of dams, levees, and flood protection structures. The agency employs about 36,000 people, including civilian and military personnel. In addition to captains, mates, and deckhands, the agency posts vacancies for drill rig operators, heavy equipment operators, engineers, laborers, writers, and contract specialists.

The agency plays a major role in marine transportation, operating canals and locks on inland waterways. They also perform dredging, wetland protection, coastal protection, and beach restoration. During emergencies, they coordinate flood control efforts with the National Weather Service, FEMA, and NOAA. [14] Naturally, federal agencies are popular with most jobseekers because of their attractive salaries and benefits.

**Dredges** Although the Army Corps of Engineers handles dredging projects throughout the United States, there are also private dredging companies that work under contract with port authorities and municipalities to keep harbors and their approaches at adequate depths. This is a very important function, and many ports would not be able to accommodate large vessels without periodic dredging of sand, mud, and silt deposits. A list of dredging contractors is provided at the end of the book.

**Marine Construction, Salvage & Environmental Remediation Vessels** Marine construction companies handle waterfront projects such as driving pilings, installing bulkheads, building piers, and demolishing existing structures. Salvage companies respond to vessels that are in peril and provide towing services, high-capacity pumps, and damage control assistance. They also remove wrecks from navigable waters.

Some general transportation companies also work in these areas. This is because the projects can require multidiscipline capabilities. If a fishing vessel runs aground, it could start out as a salvage project. However, if response personnel feel that its fuel tanks could open up under the strain of being pulled off the rocks, the scope of work for the project could change.

**Marine environmental response jobs** can often be itinerant in nature. In the photo above, BP contractors decontaminate oil booms used in remediation efforts for the *Deepwater Horizon* spill. Environmental response jobs can require being on call at all hours. Since an environmental contractor can be listed in the spill contingency plan of a tugboat company or fuel oil terminal, employees could be summoned in the middle of the night if a barge spills oil onto a creek.

That would mean deploying booms and bringing a barge alongside for transferring diesel fuel from the fishing vessel's tanks. When a single company handles such a project, it has greater control over manpower and communications, and naturally stands to make more money in the process.

**Dive Support Vessels** These vessels support commercial diving operations. They can be stationed at engineering projects near piers, bulkheads, graving docks, and power plants. The boats carry gear and provide living quarters for divers. Other work locations include sunken ships, barges, and navigational obstructions. Since divers serve the energy industry by performing underwater inspections and repairs on offshore oil rigs, many of these boats operate in the Gulf.

**Ferries** Lots of people like the idea of working on ferries because you go home at the end of the day. Work on ferries is sometimes seasonal in some regions. This means peak demands for personnel can run between Memorial Day and Labor Day, depending on tourist traffic. Therefore, some companies have to let go of non-permanent employees after September.

However, there are a considerable number of year-round operators. This area of the industry may bring to mind a small boat with a telephone booth-sized pilothouse that carries one car at a time across a lake. But some of the larger systems hire high-level mariners with unlimited licenses. Major U.S. ferry systems include the Staten Island Ferry, operated by the New York City Department of Transportation, and Washington State Ferries, run by the Washington State Department of Transportation. Additional ferry operators are listed at the end of the book.

Outside the United States, ferry operations can be a somewhat different business. Routes serving the British Isles and Scandinavian countries employ seagoing ferries that are larger than some small cruise ships. These ferries offer overnight accommodations and are known as cruiseferries.

**An impressive crew-passenger ratio** The 2,500 ton yacht *Indian Empress* is staffed by crew of 42 and carries up to 32 charter guests. Many of the megayachts and superyachts serving the charter industry today have come to symbolize exceptional levels of luxury and service. In building a yacht that measures 312 feet in length, fiberglass and wood are no longer first choices for materials. While production yachts are generally constructed of fiberglass, large yachts tend to follow contemporary shipbuilding technology. The hull of *Indian Empress* is built from steel and the upper works are aluminum. Aluminum keeps topside weight down. Three 10,000 horsepower MTU 20V1163YB93 diesels provide a top speed of 23.5 knots. [15] *Indian Empress* offers 16 cabins, an elevator, helipad, gym, and water toys that include waverunners, sea scooters, windsurfers, kayaks, and waterskis. [16]

**Water Taxis** handle the same work as ferries, which is carrying people from point A to point B. Water taxis tend to be smaller than ferries and have their routes in more sheltered waters. However, there isn't any hard-and-fast rule distinguishing the two types of vessels. Both are generally scheduled around peak commuter or tourist traffic.

**Dinner Cruise Vessels** entertain passengers on catered cruises in sheltered waters. Cruises can last from three to six hours. Therefore, the jobs are popular with people who like going home after a workday on the water. These vessels handle weddings, corporate events, and individual guests. This sector offers employment in customer service and catering-related work in addition to traditional vessel crewing positions.

**Excursion and Tour Boats** These boats take passengers on local cruises to view tourist attractions. The trips are generally several hours long. Some operators have expanded their repertoires to include sunset cruises, karaoke nights, and party charters. Sometimes the line between small ferries, water taxis, and tour boats can become blurry. Companies are constantly seeking new ways to reinvent themselves and survive in the face of a tough market. A water taxi operator might switch over to happy hour cruises in the evenings to supplement business.

**Superyachts and Megayachts** Working in this sector of the industry has its perks. You can wind up in the company of some very influential and powerful people. You could get the chance to swim and dive in beautiful tropical paradises. If you work with a friendly crew, it can mean enjoying shore excursions in some of the most exciting ports in the world.

Although the image of a yacht suggests fun and leisure, these jobs involve hard work. Workdays can be long and the tasks can be physically demanding, from keeping topsides and wooden handrails gleaming, to constantly cleaning saltwater off personal watercraft, windsurfers, and other water toys. While professionally operated vessels are generally kept clean, the level of attention to appearance aboard some large yachts can be fastidious.

In terms of scale, a yacht staff could be a crew of one, who serves as captain, mechanic, and deckhand on a Hatteras 70. This person might hold a 100 ton license and yet be humble enough to run to the supermarket for ice and beer, get into a dinghy to scrub slime off the waterline, and crawl underneath the diesels to find the source of an oil leak. The employer could be a retired couple on a modest budget. A yacht staff could also be a crew of fifty on a 280-foot superyacht, where officers hold unlimited licenses and dining room stewards wear white gloves.

**Yacht Clubs and Marinas** This sector might not be seen as part of the maritime industry because it serves the recreational boating community. However, there are openings in this area on tenders, utility boats, and mooring boats. These jobs can be seasonal or year-round, depending on the region. Tender operators drive vessels that range from 17' Boston Whaler center consoles to purpose-built inboard launches that resemble Navy whaleboats or mini-tugs.

Tender operators need a license to operate vessels carrying passengers for hire. Depending on the yacht club, tender operators are often given tips by boat owners. If a generous boat owner was appreciative of the manner in which a tender operator helped throughout the season by courteously greeting boat guests, patiently assisting older guests, and carrying ice, tips could be a significant bonus.

**Fishing Vessels** come in many different forms, including purse seiners, scallopers, shrimpers, crab boats, lobster boats, and bottom trawlers. The work schedule is governed by fishing seasons set by regulatory agencies. The location of fisheries dictates the whereabouts of job openings. In the Pacific Northwest, salmon fisheries are located off Washington, Oregon, and California.

Cod fisheries, depending on the type of cod, lie in Northern Atlantic and Northern Pacific waters. In the New England region, some of the most passionately guarded fishing grounds are those of the lobster. And in the Gulf of Mexico, shrimp comprise a major fishery.

**Record toll of $331,200 for Panama Canal transit** On May 16, 2008, the cruise ship *Disney Magic* paid the highest toll on record to use the Panama Canal. Ship operators normally bid at auction to obtain non-reserved slots for the Canal. 17 A ship that uses the canal in steaming from New York to San Francisco can shave 7,872 miles off the longer Cape Horn route around South America. On the lighter side, the lowest toll for using the Panama Canal was 36¢, paid by the adventurer Richard Halliburton when he swam the Canal in 1928. 18 The *Disney Magic* is 964 feet long and 106 feet wide, which is just inside the maximum width for transiting the Canal's 110 foot-wide locks. Built by Fincantieri Shipyards in Italy, the *Disney Magic* can carry 2,700 passengers and 950 cast members and crew. Its sister ship is the *Disney Wonder.* 19

People aren't likely to find commercial fishing jobs the way they would find jobs on cruise ships, tankers, or tugs. Fishing vessels are usually family operated, where vacancies are often filled by word of mouth, local classifieds, or relatives. However, operators of large institutionally operated fishing fleets and factory fishing vessels do solicit applicants from the public at large. Some commercial fishing positions are day jobs, while others involve extended stints at sea. The norm for the commercial fishing industry includes long hours exposed to the elements and serious occupational hazards.

**Specialized Vessels** comprise a narrow niche of the industry. These include pipe-laying vessels, cable-laying vessels, submersible heavy-lift vessels, dormitory vessels, and other purpose-built watercraft. With the current interest in alternative energy sources, an area to watch closely is that of vessels supporting the construction of offshore wind farms. Although employers in these sectors may not be as numerous as other vessel operators covered in this chapter, they shouldn't be overlooked.

This briefly outlines the various places where jobs on commercial vessels can be found. Within each of these areas, one can find different levels of specialization. For instance, the word "tugboat" suggests a hardworking, compact vessel that makes a living pushing large ships around crowded harbors. But the markets served by tugboats are multi-faceted. There are 200' salvage tugs built to tow stricken supertankers off the Cape of Good Hope, and there are 24' mini-tugs that push garbage barges around tidal basins all day long.

Tugboats and towboats serve the marine transportation sector by pushing barges carrying fuel oil, gravel, coal, bulk chemicals, and construction equipment. On inland rivers, towboats handle up to twenty or more barges in a single tow. These hardworking vessels also serve the environmental remediation industry, deploying oil containment booms and working alongside response vessels.

So while the word "tugboat" may bring to mind something like the hardworking boat in the children's book "Little Toot," it's evident that not all tugs do the same thing, and that all jobs on tugs don't necessarily involve the same duties and skills. Ship escort work can require proficiency with azimuthing drives in herding giant tankers through narrowly dredged channels. Towing work can mean dealing with unwieldy barges that sometimes have minds of their own. Ship assist work can require the ability to gently coax 80,000 ton container ships into tight slips without putting holes in their sides.

Inland towing work can chew through relief deckhands in the labor-intensive process of breaking down large tows to pass through canals and locks. With so many different types of work involving tugs, one realizes it's hard to be good at everything. There are people with years of experience who are versatile in multiple areas. But that's not the point.

The point is that even when classified ads use the same job titles, the duties and responsibilities can differ from one type of vessel to another. The skill sets for a mate on a crab fishing boat are very different from those for a mate on a towing vessel. Certain skills are universal, such as seamanship or navigation. However, different types of vessels conduct different missions, which can make for different duties, even when the jobs are identified by the same title. This may become clearer after reading the next two chapters, which describe the jobs that arise in the industry.

So You Want to Work on a Boat

# What Positions Are Out There? Inland & Coastal Vessels

The use of job titles on commercial vessels can seem confusing at times. On tugs, ferries, and offshore supply vessels, you'll see about half a dozen basic job titles used. On cruise ships, you'll see over fifty. All these different job titles aren't always generic throughout the industry. Adding to the confusion, people sometimes use titles loosely.

**Inland and Coastal Vessels** On inland and coastal vessels such as tugboats, you'll see help wanted ads for the positions of captain, mate, engineer, and deckhand (or seaman). Larger tugs employ dedicated cooks and additional personnel, such as DDEs and QMEDs. On smaller tugs, cooking and cleaning duties may be assumed by deckhands. On a commuter ferry, the entire crew roster may consist of a captain and deckhand. On commercial fishing vessels, there is generally a captain, mate, and several deckhands.

Larger fishing vessels may additionally employ dedicated engine room personnel, additional deckhands, and fish processing personnel. The job description for a *mate* can differ significantly between large ships and small inland vessels. On large ships, a mate is one of three deck officers. But on smaller vessels, there is usually only one mate, who is second in command to the captain. Let's go through an overview of the positions out there. Maybe a good place to start is with the deckhand. This is a primary entry-level opportunity for many newcomers.

**A note about job titles** It isn't always easy to apply generic titles to jobs on commercial vessels. Titles are sometimes used loosely, and can differ from one type of vessel to another. A person referred to as a *mate* on a party fishing boat like the one pictured above might handle duties that resemble those of a deckhand on a coastal tanker. This could mean something very different than *mate* in the context of a *first mate* on a 50,000 ton container ship. Adding to the confusion, some job titles happen to be Coast Guard ratings. For instance, a certain number of *deckhands* on a tug might need to be *able seamen* for a particular voyage. Also, there are job titles with more than one meaning. Consider the title *pilot*. A towboat *pilot* alternates watches with the captain on inland vessels and handles duties similar to a *mate* on a tugboat. However, a *pilot* is also someone who helps vessels navigate unfamiliar waters. Therefore, it's important to keep in mind that this discussion of job titles is a generalized overview.

**Deckhand** A deckhand is the "grunt" of the industry. The job often involves handling heavy lines to secure vessels to docks or to one another. On tugboats and towboats, deckhands lash together barges to form tows. On ferries, they handle boarding ramps and cordon off restricted areas when the boat is underway. On fishing vessels, they handle nets, lobster or crab pots, paravanes, and outriggers.

Deckhands must be physically fit and strong. They should be able to throw lines with reasonable accuracy and retrieve lines thrown by other deckhands. They need to be able to lift heavy objects, climb ladders, kneel down to open hatches, and perform other physically demanding tasks throughout the course of work. It isn't an ideal job for a middle-aged person who wants to embark on a journey of self-discovery on the water after working at a comfortable desk job. The job requires stamina, as assignments or projects on the water can take longer than scheduled.

The elements can be harsh upon the deckhand. Mother Nature can be merciless with brutal sun in the summer and stabbing cold winds in the winter. Deckhands might wear foul weather gear over thick sweaters in the winter, and T-shirts and shorts in the summer. Working as a deckhand is one of the most dangerous occupations in the world.

Deckhands can fall overboard while setting up barges for tows. They can be washed over the side while hauling crab pots. Such hazards are intensified by the fact that in rough seas, severe winds, or darkness, it's easy to fall overboard without shipmates noticing. This is especially true on small vessels with only five or six people aboard. As a side note, commercial mariners on any vessel must be extra attentive to each other's whereabouts in dangerous sea conditions.

The day-to-day duties of a deckhand can be diverse. When things are slow, deckhands may chip rust or apply paint. They may lubricate winches. They may inspect hydraulic hoses for leaks. They may inventory safety gear. Operating in the harsh environment of saltwater and sea air, equipment needs constant attention. Junior deckhands may be assigned to cleaning work areas and living quarters.

**Edison Chouest Offshore** operates tugboats but also handles a diverse range of other marine services. It has over 200 vessels that range from 87 feet in length to over 360 feet in length. This includes light construction vessels, anchor handling towing supply vessels, multi-purpose supply vessels, platform supply vessels, oil spill response vessels, fast supply vessels, tractor tugs, and specialty vessels. In the photo above, *C-Tractor 14* assists the *USS Warrior*, a mine countermeasure ship. *C-Tractor 14* is operated by Alpha Marine Services, a subsidiary of Edison Chouest Offshore. The z-drive tug is powered by twin Caterpillar diesels, giving it a total of 4,000 horsepower. [20, 21]

Deckhands can be called upon to help a cook carry groceries or help the chief engineer carry spare diesel parts. In crowded waterways where an empty barge obstructs visibility from the wheelhouse, deckhands can be sent forward to serve as lookouts. If a captain or mate is the mentoring type, a deckhand can be called to the wheelhouse to learn about plotting a course or reading a navigational chart.

A mate could invite a deckhand to operate "the sticks." Sticks are levers that control rudder movements. On certain types of vessels, they are more practical than traditional ship's wheels because it takes less travel to go from full starboard to full port. Going to the other end of the spectrum of jobs on commercial vessels brings us to the position of captain.

**Captain** The captain is master of a vessel. He or she makes all command decisions. Ultimate responsibility for the safety of the crew and vessel rests on the shoulders of the captain. On inland and coastal vessels, the captain generally shares watchstanding duties with the mate.

Captains hold Coast Guard licenses, ranging from 25 tons on smaller vessels to 100 ton, 200 ton, 500 ton, 1600 ton, all the way to unlimited tonnage on larger vessels. Captains on small uninspected vessels that carry passengers for hire may hold an *operator uninspected power vessel* (OUPV), or *six-pack* license. An example is a charter fishing boat captain.

On large tugs, captains often hold a 1600 ton license. Although the title of captain is sometimes used informally, the position is a serious career milestone that can take years to attain. Captains on inland and coastal vessels often start out as deckhands and assume positions of increasing responsibility, while attaining higher grade licenses and endorsements along the way.

The position of captain might be seen as the job with the best view and best single cabin on the boat. However, a captain is in the unenviable position of having to make important decisions, such as selecting voyage routes, selecting times and tides to negotiate inlets, making calls on the weather, recommending certain employees for promotion, and sometimes recommending others for termination.

This means that in addition to navigation, seamanship, meteorology, and collision regs, captains must be somewhat familiar with practical maritime law, employment law, and conflict resolution. A captain must balance the morale of a crew with the expectations and budget of the home office. It can take some social skills to pull that off in a way that establishes authority while maintaining a pleasant work atmosphere.

**Moran Towing Corporation** provides towing and transportation services on the East and West Coasts, Great Lakes, Gulf of Mexico, and other regions. It operates 95 tugs and 30 barges, including tractor tugs and articulated barge units. In the photo above, the tug *Bart Turecamo* assists the *USS Kauffman* during Philadelphia Fleet Week in 2008. *Bart Turecamo* was built in 1968 and exhibits the classic lines of a traditional tugboat. Weighing in at 266 gross tons and measuring 96.6 feet in length, it is powered by twin Fairbanks Morse diesels that produce 2,880 horsepower. 22, 23

It's easy for someone gazing at a towboat from shore to see a captain in the wheelhouse and think, "That's what I want to do!" But there are many aspects of the job that most people don't think about. A captain has to fill out a logbook during each watch. A captain must ensure that a vessel is operated in accordance with Coast Guard regulations, stability letters, environmental regulations, employer's standard operating procedures, and human resources policies.

**Some people could be squeamish about working around hazardous chemicals.** For them, chemical transport might not be the best line of work. Certain vessels and barges are designed to transport bulk sulfuric acid, hydrochloric acid, sodium hydroxide, paraxylene, anhydrous ammonia, and other chemicals. Such cargos can present health hazards through skin contact or inhalation. There are people who don't have a problem with putting on protective gear to enter a tank or clean up a chemical spill. However, for those with pressing concerns about working around such substances, there are other types of vessels on which they could be more comfortable. Chemical transport vessels and barges are unique in that their cargo holds, piping systems, valves, and pumps are specially lined to be impervious to the corrosive and reactive characteristics of these types of cargos.

Captains must answer for delays in arrival, or damage to cargo. Captains must fill out performance assessments. Select captains must train and examine crew members slated for promotion. This is an especially important facet of the job in regions where experienced captains and mates are nearing retirement age. So while the view from the wheelhouse or bridge may seem like a covetable one, people should realize that there are many stressful responsibilities and obligations that come with the territory.

**Pilots** are officers who serve on towing vessels, often in inland waters. A pilot reports to the captain, and alternates watchstanding duties with the captain. The duties of a pilot are similar to those of a mate on a tugboat. Pilots are sometimes hired for a particular voyage, and are called *trip pilots* in those instances. This type of pilot is not to be confused with the marine pilot who assists a vessel's deck officers in transiting unfamiliar waters.

**Mate** On inland and coastal vessels, mates supervise unlicensed crewmembers, allowing captains to tend to managerial and administrative duties such as preparing for safety inspections, writing incident reports, applying for fishing permits, reviewing logbooks, developing training schedules, and tending to human resources matters. On inland and coastal vessels, mates generally alternate six-hour watches with captains. Mates tend to navigation, maintenance, and cargo operations. Like captains, mates can be assigned to train selected crew members.

The boundaries of a mate's authority are generally governed by experience. If a mate is new and a captain is highly experienced, the captain may supervise certain aspects of vessel operations while assessing the mate's leadership abilities. Interestingly, some mates hold licenses as masters and continue to sail as mates. It may depend upon their personal choice, or the availability of captain positions within a company.

**Apprentice Mate** This position is seen on towing vessels. It describes someone qualified to stand watches in the wheelhouse, while training under the direct supervision of a licensed master, mate, or pilot on towing vessels. Such a person is also called a *steersman.*

**Ballast Control Operator** This person is responsible for operating ballast systems on mobile offshore drilling units, or MODUs. These systems can be complex, requiring practical naval architectural insight into how vessel trim and stability are affected by shifting ballast.

Trim refers to fore and aft changes in the attitude of a vessel, while stability refers to port and starboard changes in the attitude of a vessel. Placing too much ballast on the right side of a vessel will result in a starboard list, which is a change in *stability*. Hitting a reef and flooding the forepeak will result in a settling of the bow, which is a change in *trim*. Ballast control operators are also called BCOs.

**Barge Supervisor** This person is responsible for watertight integrity, mooring gear, towing gear, emergency gear, and other equipment on mobile offshore drilling units. Vacancies for barge supervisors and BCOs generally arise in the oil, gas, and energy exploration industry in the Gulf and other energy hubs.

**Engineering personnel** Engineering personnel operate and maintain main engines, generator sets, and the various systems and equipment for fuel polishing, fuel transfer, lube oil, fire protection, electrical distribution, compressed air, service water, sanitation, heating, air conditioning, and ventilation.

On large ships, engineering officers generally hold unlimited horsepower licenses. On coastal and inland vessels, **engineering officers** might hold limited horsepower licenses. They could have endorsements in offshore supply vessels, mobile offshore drilling units, or uninspected fishing vessels. On vessels without requirements for dedicated engineering personnel, deckhands are sometimes relegated to engine room duties and are called *deckineers*.

**A special relationship** Commercial mariners are familiar with the role of the U.S. Coast Guard in terms of law enforcement, safety inspections, incident reporting, and licensing. While mariners realize that running afoul of regulations can result in disciplinary action, prosecution, or suspension of a license, they also appreciate the role of the Coast Guard as a watchful guardian. When a vessel on the Bering Sea succumbs to flooding or fire, it's Coast Guard search and rescue teams who climb aboard Jayhawk helicopters at 2:00 am, braving snowstorms to pluck mariners from bone-chilling seas. In the photo above, a deckhand prepares to unload a crab pot with the *USCGC Sherman* (WHEC-720) in the background.

The **designated duty engineer, or DDE**, handles the operation of engines and auxiliary systems. On vessels where the engine room is not attended full-time, the DDE could be the sole engineering department person on board. Designated duty engineers must pass a Coast Guard exam, rated in 1,000 horsepower, 4,000 horsepower, or unlimited horsepower capacities. They may be assisted in watchstanding and maintenance duties by additional personnel, who could be qualified or non-qualified ratings.

Qualified ratings are known as QMEDs (qualified members of the engineering department).

**Keeping provisions fresh at sea** has historically been a challenge for cooks on all types of vessels. Although modern commercial vessels usually have generous freezer spaces, keeping provisions fresh aboard a World War II submarine was difficult. Before setting out to sea, U-boat crews would stuff food into every available corner, including toilet spaces. A voyage started with fresh meat, sausage, bread, and fruit. However, in the damp confines of a submarine, bread soon sprouted white fungi. Crews nicknamed the loaves of bread "rabbits," because the fungi gave them a white fuzzy appearance. After all the fresh food was eaten, the crew turned to canned goods. Because these took on the tinge of the submarine's odors, the crew called the fare "diesel food." 24

A century earlier, whaling ship crews came up with a more brutal solution to the age-old problem of keeping provisions fresh at sea. In the Galapagos Islands, they discovered "live" food in the form of tortoises. An account from a whaling ship captain in the 1800s describes the process of harvesting these gentle animals. "We went hunting them every day for a week, and as they are so clumsy and move so slow, made it an easy matter to capture them... We put them on deck and between decks, and let them crawl around as they chose. It was all of six months before they were all gone. I never knew one to eat or drink a drop while they were on board, and yet they looked as fat as a ball of butter when they were killed." 25

**Qualified members of the engineering department** serve on inland and ocean-going vessels alike. To serve as a QMED, someone must satisfy sea time requirements and pass a Coast Guard exam. There are different QMED ratings, which include engineman, deck engine mechanic, pumpman, machinist, electrician, deck engineer, refrigerating engineer, junior engineer, oiler, and fireman/watertender.

It generally takes 6 months of sea time to sit for one of these exams, with a few exceptions. This information appears on the U.S. Coast Guard's National Maritime Center website. The *Frequently Asked Questions* section provides detailed information on sea time requirements, at http://www.uscg.mil/nmc/faq/merchant_mariners_credentials.asp.

All of these engineering department positions are physically demanding. On vessels involving watchstanding routines, this can mean being stationed in an engine room and reading gauges to monitor circulating water temperatures, exhaust pressures, engine rpms, electrical system voltages, amperages, and other operating parameters.

These spaces are generally loud and hot. The jobs require the ability to move around and climb ladders to inspect equipment. Engineering personnel periodically check the levels of diesel fuel in various tanks. They also make rounds to check temperatures and vibration levels of bearings on pumps, motors, and compressors to ensure proper operation. As the need arises, lubricants and coolants are added.

There are additional duties performed by engineering personnel. It isn't easy to draw the line and say "this job" or "that job" is off-limits for an engineering officer... he would definitely assign something like that to a newbie. Different officers have their own philosophies about running their engine rooms, with many of them just rolling up their sleeves and working alongside subordinates.

Some of these day-to-day duties include cleaning seawater strainers, performing oil changes, cleaning heat exchangers, plugging leaking tubes in heat exchangers, replacing small motors, and conducting tests on equipment. As for major repairs, those are usually handled in shipyards under the supervision of a company port engineer.

**Tankerman** Let's climb out of the engine room for a moment and get some fresh air up on deck. We'll need it because we'll be going below again to see what a tankerman does. Under the supervision of the captain or mate, tankermen load and offload liquid cargos.

Tankermen must understand the operation of cargo pumps, valves, and piping to do this safely. Typical liquid cargos include fuel oil, home heating oil, diesel fuel, kerosene, solvents, and bulk chemicals. They must have an appreciation of how cargo transfers affect trim and stability. Tankermen can face occupational hazards in entering empty cargo holds and confined spaces. The job is particularly difficult in warm regions.

Wearing respirators and other protective equipment on a hot summer day to enter a tank for inspection can be uncomfortable. Ladder rungs and handrails can be slippery from residual cargo. Cargo vapors can cause irritation. Worse, vapors could be combustible or flammable in some cases.

The position of tankerman carries heavy responsibilities. Making a mistake in opening or closing valves can cause cargo to overflow and spill overboard. This could result in a visit from government agencies that have the authority to prosecute such incidents as crimes.

**Cook** As the name suggests, a cook prepares meals for the crew. Although cooks don't stand fixed watches, the workday for a dedicated cook is a long one. It means getting a pot of coffee going early in the morning, fixing three square meals a day for a hardworking crew, and making sure that snacks or treats are available for people going on or coming off watch.

Since cooks shop for groceries with money allocated by a company budget, they must be familiar with prices at supermarkets and warehouse stores. They must be able to plan menus several weeks ahead of time, appreciating which fruits and vegetables spoil before others, which items can be frozen, and which items last indefinitely.

It can take imagination and creativity to whip up meals that are nutritious and filling, while staying within the home office's budget. It's a big responsibility to keep ten or twenty people happy with food for several weeks at a stretch. Shipboard work is repetitive and tedious. After a voyage drags on and crewmembers start counting down days to get home, a cook can become the bright spot for everyone on board.

Cooks sometimes make things fun by having barbeques or pizza nights once a week. To the extent possible, some cooks try to accommodate special needs of crewmembers. Cooks may be self-trained or institutionally trained. A close land-based equivalent is a short order cook at a diner.

**Chef** A chef prepares meals on yachts, cruise ships, and other luxury vessels. Depending on the setting, the position can require restaurant or hotel kitchen experience. Guests on megayachts expect the finest gourmet meals and wines. It can be tricky to describe the difference between a chef and a cook. People might think of a chef as a cook who wears a fancy white hat. Another impression might be that a cook breaks open four eggs at a time with both hands on an ocean-going tug, while a chef knows the secret to preparing the perfect soufflé aboard a luxury yacht.

In terms of competence, both positions require strong knowledge of safe food handling practices and kitchen sanitation. The distinction between cooks and chefs is usually based on education and experience. With cruise lines, job requirements for chefs are quite clear in terms of culinary school credentials and high-end hotel restaurant experience. However, on smaller vessels, it can sometimes be a matter of what the person in the galley calls himself. In other words, "I am a chef... not a cook!"

**Stewards** take care of dining room service, housekeeping, and room service. It's a physically demanding job on any ship. But on luxury megayachts and superyachts, stewards can be expected to maintain the highest standards of customer service. And behind the scenes, stewards work hard in moving dining room furniture, vacuuming carpets, scrubbing floors, and keeping fine china and silverware spotless.

So You Want to Work on a Boat

# What Positions Are Out There?
# Ocean-Going Vessels

The subject of job descriptions is covered here in two chapters. The previous chapter discussed jobs on inland and coastal vessels, while this chapter deals with positions on larger ocean-going vessels. Splitting things this way doesn't exactly work out perfectly, since there are jobs that are common to both large and small vessels. However, this format was chosen to provide better guidance in terms of conducting job searches based on the type of vessel one has in mind. It was also done to make it easier for readers to gather *keywords* they could use for online job searches.

On large cargo ships, typical crew sizes range from fifteen to thirty people. This includes container ships, car carriers, bulk carriers, and tankers. Entry-level positions include ordinary seamen, in the deck department; wipers, in the engine department; and food handlers, in the steward's department.

**Bosuns (or Boatswains)** ordinarily supervise and train unlicensed crewmembers in the deck department. You might compare them to chief petty officers in the Navy, who are often respected for their extensive shipboard experience.

**Able Seamen** are higher level seamen than ordinary seamen. They may be assigned duties such as steering a vessel, plotting courses, and splicing wire rope. Depending on manpower needs, they may also work alongside ordinary seamen in chipping, painting, and maintaining cargo handling gear.

**It's hard to imagine that only 15 people run a ship** that's longer than some World War II battleships. This is the result of automation in the engine room and bridge. The *Don Quijote* is a PCTC, or Pure Car Truck Carrier. The 28,141 ton vessel can carry 7,200 cars. A relatively new ship, built in 1998 by Daewoo Shipbuilding and Marine Engineering, the *Don Quijote* measures 748 feet in length, 106 feet in width, and has a draft of 36 feet. The 19,698 horsepower vessel is owned by Wallenius Lines and is managed by Wallenius Marine. Such a design is the most effective configuration for moving rolling stock, and is also used for transporting military equipment. Wallenius was founded in 1934. Together with its subsidiaries, it operates some 135 vessels and transports more than seven million cars annually. 26

**Ordinary Seamen** are comparable to deckhands on smaller vessels. They handle lines. They chip rust and apply paint. They sweep, mop, and clean shipboard areas. They perform basic maintenance on lifeboats, winches, and other equipment. They work under the guidance of bosuns and deck officers. An ordinary seaman can advance to the position of able seaman.

It can be difficult to draw the line where the duties of an ordinary seaman end and an able seaman begin. When preparing a container ship for sea, both can work alongside each other in setting up lashing gear. On a cruise ship, both may perform maintenance duties on lifeboats. And again, this is one of those areas that can be a little confusing because job titles used in classified ads might not correspond with the exact terms for these ratings, as outlined below.

Able seamen are qualified deck ratings just as QMEDs are qualified engineering department ratings. They can be able seamen-unlimited, able seamen-limited, able seamen-special, able seamen-mobile offshore unit, able seamen-offshore supply vessel, able seamen-fishing industry, able seamen-sail, lifeboatmen, or lifeboatmen-offshore mobile unit. Each rating has its own sea time requirements, ranging from 360 days to 1080 days.

This might be more information than necessary for someone who just wants to get a general overview of shipboard jobs. But some readers may want additional detail. This information appears in the U.S. Coast Guard's National Maritime Center website. For a complete outline of sea time requirements, go to the *Frequently Asked Questions* section of the National Maritime Center site, at http://www.uscg.mil/nmc/faq/merchant_mariners_credentials.asp.

In searching for a job, you're likely to see job listings for *deckhands* with operators of tugs, ferries, and other inland vessels. With cruise ships and large cargo ships, you're likely to see classified ads for *seamen* or *able seamen*. Employment ads may also use the term *able-bodied seamen*. Some companies will be precise in using these terms for their job postings, while others may use the terms loosely.

**Food Handlers** are entry-level personnel in the steward's department. The steward's department handles meals and housekeeping services. Food handlers assist cooks and chefs by bringing food up from freezer spaces, chopping vegetables, washing salads, preparing sandwiches, cleaning workstations, and handling other tasks. The job descriptions provided in the previous chapter for **cooks** and **chefs** can be applied to large cargo vessels as well.

**Shipboard operations** on large vessels fall under two major groups, being the deck department and the engineering department. There are other departments that work around the clock, such as security and medical departments on cruise ships. But *deck* and *engine* are the traditionally means of separating things for the purposes of vessel crewing, educational curricula, and Coast Guard licenses.

Deck personnel handle navigation and cargo operations. Engineering personnel operate and maintain main engines and auxiliaries. The deck department traditionally consists of a captain, first officer, second officer, third officer, bosuns, able seamen, and ordinary seamen. The engineering department traditionally consists of a chief engineer, first assistant engineer, second assistant engineer, third assistant engineer, QMEDs, and wipers.

**Captain** On large ships, a captain is in overall command of everyone, directly or indirectly, which holds true for inland or coastal vessels as well. A captain on a large ship typically holds an unlimited tonnage master license. This means years of sea time as third officer, second officer, and first officer before becoming captain.

The larger the vessel, the more managerial and administrative in nature a captain's duties are. On inland and coastal vessels, a captain generally alternates six-hour watches with the mate. On ocean-going vessels, a captain does not stand watches, unless covering for a sick deck officer. A captain is also called a *master*.

**Working aboard the *SS United States*** would have been a crowning achievement in the career of a professional mariner in the 1950s and '60s. Launched in 1952 at Newport News Shipbuilding, the vessel possessed spectacular speed and unprecedented safety features. But the introduction of jetliners proved to be the undoing of such magnificent vessels. Although its 248,000 horsepower engines enabled the *United States* to walk away from fast destroyers without breaking a sweat, such things would mean little to cruise ship passengers today. Nowadays, it's about shipboard waterparks, rock climbing walls, shopping malls, casinos, and endless sushi. Nevertheless, it must have been exhilarating to step out onto one of Big U's bridge wings as a watch officer on a crisp fall night in the North Atlantic and feel a 40 knot headwind in your face. In the photo above, the *United States* is in the background. The ship in the foreground is the *SS America*.

It isn't uncommon for someone to hold a master license, but sail as a senior officer. This may be because more job opportunities materialize for first officers and second officers than for captains. The term *license* is used on U.S. vessels. Other countries may use the term *certificate of competency*.

**First Officer** The first officer is also called a first mate. In some instances, the title chief officer or chief mate is used. First officers are traditionally in charge of cargo operations. This is an important function because improperly loaded cargo can cause a ship to hog or sag. Hogging is a condition where a ship bends like a limp noodle held up in the center by a pencil. Sagging is the opposite, where a ship is bowed downwards in the center, as in the case of someone sitting in the middle of a hammock. Either condition is bad for the structural integrity of a ship, which is essentially a giant box beam.

**Second Officer** The second officer is also called a second mate. Second officers are traditionally in charge of navigation. Shipboard navigation technology has seen tremendous development in recent decades. Traditional paper nautical charts have progressively been replaced by electronic charts. This is not just a whim of fancy. IMO, the International Maritime Organization, has mandated deck officer competence with electronic charts on an international level. Second officers oversee the updating of electronic navigation systems.

**Third Officer** The third officer is also called a third mate. Third officers are traditionally in charge of lifeboats and lifesaving equipment. This includes holding lifeboat drills to ensure that crews are familiar with their lifeboat stations and duties. It also means inspecting lifeboats and related equipment for compliance with safety regulations. This area is the focus of SOLAS, the International Convention for the Safety of Life at Sea.

**Chief Engineer** This officer is the head of the engineering department. On large vessels, a chief engineer doesn't generally stand watches, unless covering for an engineering officer who is sick. A chief engineer's duties are managerial in nature, and include planning budgets, overseeing preventive maintenance programs, and assigning projects to engineering officers. In recent years, chief engineers have placed greater emphasis on compliance with shipboard environmental regulations.

**Working aboard a commercial vessel fosters a healthy respect for fire safety**. There is no fire department 100 miles out at sea. Yet, there are countless ways for shipboard fires to get the better of a vessel. New mariners are introduced to a concept known as the "fire triangle." This means that a fire requires three elements, being fuel, heat, and oxygen. In the converse, removing one of the elements should extinguish a fire... or at least serve toward extinguishing it. In the photo above, rescuers douse flames on the deck of a tanker. A major objective in such a situation is to cut off fuel supply. This eliminates the "fuel" leg of the fire triangle. The continuous stream of cold seawater serves to cool deck plates, thus removing the "heat" element of the triangle.

**First Assistant Engineers** are also referred to as 1st A/Es. They're traditionally in charge of main engines, which can be steam turbines, diesels, or gas turbines. First assistant engineers monitor the operation of all important machinery from a soundproof control room, periodically making rounds to physically inspect pumps, motors, compressors, and other equipment. It's one thing to read a computer display of temperatures and pressures, but it's another to make a round to check for leaks, fires, or other safety hazards. Like the other engineering officers described here, they will fill out a logbook during each watch and handle any tasks or projects assigned by the chief engineer.

**Second Assistant Engineers** are also referred to as $2^{nd}$ A/Es. They are traditionally in charge of main boilers and bunkering (fueling) operations. As with the other engineering officers, watchstanding time is divided between the control room and machinery spaces. On steam-driven ships, one of the important duties of the second assistant engineer is to monitor boiler water chemistry. Bunkering is also a critical operation because it presents the risk of petroleum releases onto navigable waters, which can result in environmental damage and enforcement actions from regulatory agencies.

**Third Assistant Engineers** are also referred to as $3^{rd}$ A/Es. They are traditionally in charge of auxiliaries and sewage treatment plants. Auxiliaries include refrigeration systems, desalination systems, water filtration systems, heating ventilation & air conditioning systems, and other miscellaneous equipment and systems. Watchstanding time is divided between the control room and machinery spaces, as with the other engineering officers. All of these engineering officers perform repairs and maintenance. They also act as mentors for cadets and students who are assigned to a ship.

On large ships, engineering officers generally hold unlimited horsepower licenses, endorsed in diesel, steam, or gas turbines. Gas turbines are popular for military vessels, such as frigates, destroyers, and cruisers. They deliver tremendous horsepower for their weight and offer quick acceleration. Although civilian marine engineers may deal with gas turbine emergency generators, they don't often work with gas turbines as prime movers, since most civilian ships don't need to reach speeds of 30 knots.

Steam was once a predominant prime mover in the U.S. merchant marine. Today, large low-speed diesels are favored because of their high reliability and good fuel economy. Diesels have also made the job of the marine engineer less complex in terms of plant operations. Gone are the days of lighting off boilers four hours before sailing time to raise steam for turbines. Steam is still found in a few places, such as the *USNS Mercy* or *USNS Comfort*, Navy hospital ships operated by the U.S. Military Sealift Command.

Engineering officers are assisted in watchstanding and maintenance duties by wipers and **qualified members of the engineering department**, or **QMEDs**. As mentioned in the previous chapter, QMEDs include enginemen, pumpmen, firemen/watertenders, and oilers. They may also be assisted by day workers such as electricians and plumbers on larger ships.

**Wipers** are entry-level engine department personnel. They make rounds of machinery spaces and report irregularities to engineering officers. They clean machinery and dispose of rags, rubbish, and other fire hazards. They lubricate engines, pumps, motors, and compressors. They operate valves and measure tank levels. **Oilers** handle similar duties, but are senior to wipers. Oilers, who are also QMEDs, are generally assigned tasks that require greater experience or judgment.

The most diverse selection of jobs on large vessels can be found in the cruise industry. Back in the seventies and eighties, there was a television series called *The Love Boat*. In addition to being a family favorite on Saturday nights, the show provided a glimpse into the organizational structure of a cruise ship, albeit on a small level.

**Much of the electronic technology** we enjoy today was not around in the 1970s... the Internet, affordable personal computers, and e-mail. Something else that wasn't around back then was the position of *shipboard information technology (IT) officer.* This "techie" is vital to the operation of a large cruise ship. Crewmembers and passengers depend on a ship's network for operations, billing, and communications. Imagine life at sea without e-mails or internet access. That's the way it was in the golden age of transatlantic liners, such as the *Queen Mary*, pictured above. Back in the 1930s, passengers were content enough to watch a small replica of the ship move across an art deco map of the North Atlantic over the course of a voyage. As for high-tech communications, there were ship's postcards! But things have changed a great deal since those days, bringing about the need for high-tech personnel such as shipboard IT officers.

*Captain* Merrill Stubing was the top deck officer. *Bartender* Isaac Washington mixed drinks in the catering and beverage department. *Purser* Burl "Gopher" Smith attended to a myriad of shipboard problems. *Cruise Director* Julie McCoy arranged fun-filled events in the activities department. *Doctor* Adam Bricker tended to sprains and bruises in the medical department. This cheerful group was always there for passengers on the *Pacific Princess*.

Cruise ships essentially follow the same organizational structure found in the deck and engine departments of other large vessels. However, in addition to the traditional titles used for the common deck and engine officer positions, some cruise lines use different terms in certain instances. These may include navigation officer or staff chief engineer, among others. To figure out the traditional equivalent of such titles, look at the licensing requirements listed in a cruise line's job descriptions.

A unique cruise ship position is that of **safety officer**. Often a first mate by training, this officer focuses on lifeboat drills, fire safety, and other high priority issues related to keeping thousands of passengers safe. Another unique cruise ship position is the **staff captain**. The captain on a cruise ship is like a corporate CEO, dealing with the "big picture."

The staff captain serves as operational head of the deck department, supervising deck officers and carrying out the duties of a traditional captain aboard any other large ship. The captain remains in the position of holding primary accountability to the cruise line's main office. In addition to its deck officers, a large cruise ship will have a well-sized complement of bosuns, able seamen, and ordinary seamen.

Although the organizational structure of the engineering department on a cruise ship is similar to that of any other large vessel, there's a difference in numbers. A cruise ship carrying 3,000 passengers requires a larger staff to serve the increased electrical, refrigeration, water, sewage treatment, and air conditioning demands.

Large cruise ships may employ **refrigeration officers**, whose duties involve operation and maintenance of refrigeration and air conditioning equipment. Large cruise ships also employ **electrical officers**, dedicated to serving the power demands of propulsion drive motors and passenger staterooms. Cruise ships also carry additional mechanics, plumbers, and electricians to keep so many elevators, sinks, and lights running properly.

The **environmental officer** is a relative newcomer to the playing field, when you consider that some of the jobs described here have been around for centuries, in form at least. This person is responsible for ensuring a cruise ship's compliance with regulations for incineration, waste disposal, spill reporting, and air emissions.

Shipboard waste streams include solid wastes, engine room solvents, photographic chemicals, sewage water discharges (black water), and non-sewage water discharges (grey water). The environmental officer is responsible for the proper management of these waste streams in accordance with MARPOL and other regulations.

Cruise ships can carry one or more **security officers**. Large cruise ships easily employ over a thousand people. Add to that three thousand or more passengers, and one can appreciate the potential for accidents, thefts, sexual assaults, disorderly conduct, and other security breaches. Security officers maintain order and investigate crimes and accidents.

Investigation involves interviewing witnesses, obtaining statements, taking photographs, and writing reports. This serves to control a cruise line's exposure if sued by injured passengers. The security officer is assisted by **surveillance specialists** and **security specialists**.

On large cargo ships, deck and engine personnel nearly make up the entire ship's complement. But on cruise ships, these two departments are a very small part of the entire crew roster. Cruise ships can be thought of as floating hotels that travel from one port to another. As with any major hotel, a large staff is needed for restaurants, cocktail lounges, housekeeping, entertainment, casinos, youth activities, and water activities.

The **catering department**, or **culinary department**, is responsible for preparing thousands of meals on a daily basis for passengers and crewmembers. On reputable cruise lines, meals must be appetizing, interesting, and nutritious. Cruise ships also provide specialty dining in restaurants that aren't part of the included passenger fare. Cruise lines look for serious backgrounds to fill senior positions in this department. This generally means education at a culinary school and hotel restaurant experience. Commonly used titles include **executive chef**, **sous chef**, **senior chef**, and **chef**.

Executive chefs and sous chefs are senior level chefs who supervise other members of the culinary staff. Although such chefs are versed in creating gourmet entrees, the ability to produce them on a scale for thousands of passengers requires strong supervisory and organizational skills. Cruise ships often use a system of stations, e.g., salad stations, soup stations, desert stations, etc. to keep up with the high volume of food required.

Galley sanitation is important aboard all vessels. However, on cruise ships, the consequences of poor sanitation can be costly in terms of productivity, reputation, and lawsuits. The prevention of gastrointestinal diseases caused by Norovirus, Salmonella, E. coli, and other sources is a high priority for culinary department personnel.

Because of the competitive nature of the cruise industry, many cruise lines hire sushi chefs, teppanyaki chefs, pastry chefs, and other specialists who concentrate in a particular area. The larger and more luxurious the cruise line, the greater the lengths to which it will go to impress passengers to develop loyalty to a brand.

**A report card for cruise ships** The importance of thoroughly washing salads and disinfecting galley work areas is obviously an essential part of health and sanitation at sea. But it's important for another reason, which is to attain a good report card with the Centers for Disease Control and Prevention. The CDC keeps records for the cruise industry through its Vessel Sanitation Program. Cruise lines that participate in the program must report the total number of gastrointestinal illness cases evaluated by the medical staff prior to arrival at a U.S. port. If the number of sickened passengers exceeds 2% of the total roster for passengers and crew, a separate notification must be made. 27 Naturally, these are statistics that cruise lines strive to avoid.

The culinary department also employs **bakers, food managers**, **maitre d's**, **waiters**, **waitresses**, **dishwashers**, and **storekeepers**. Readers need no explanation regarding the duties of people who handle these jobs. However, as mentioned earlier, the positions can involve very tough work schedules.

Closely tied to the culinary department, the beverage department employs **beverage managers**, **bartenders**, and **assistant bartenders**. Managers supervise bartenders and track inventories for liquor, wine, beer, and other drinks. Bartenders serve drinks to passengers, relying on tips to supplement their base pay. Therefore, a cheerful disposition can affect the bottom line for one's wages.

A large cruise ship can have many bartenders throughout various passenger lounges and swimming areas. In addition to its bartenders, cruise ships may employ **wine stewards**, who make recommendations to guests about what kind of wine to order with a meal. Since bottled wine can be expensive and people watch their money closely these days, this position can require persuasive sales abilities.

Large cruise ships derive a significant portion of their revenues from onboard casinos. Cruise lines seek out candidates with experience from established shoreside casinos. Some of the job openings that regularly appear in this department include **cashiers**, **dealers**, **slot technicians**, and **surveillance specialists**.

Cruise lines also employ **accountants**, **bookkeepers**, and **pursers** to oversee financial operations on a vessel. As with any large hotel, passengers can have questions about charges on their bills. In addition, time sheets and wages for ship's personnel must be managed at sea.

Service and specialty personnel include **massage therapists**, **spa treatment specialists**, **hair stylists**, **beauticians**, and **manicurists**. These employees provide services for well-being, relaxation, beauty, and style. Like many other cruise ship positions, they are essentially shoreside jobs that have been transplanted into shipboard settings.

The entertainment department provides stage shows, music concerts, and other activities for passengers. These positions are often filled through recruitment events, such as job fairs and auditions. They include **dancers**, **singers**, **musicians**, **magicians**, **jugglers**, **ventriloquists**, **comedians**, and other **stage performers**. This department also has regular openings for **DJs**, **sound technicians**, and **lighting technicians**.

Cruise lines realize that when you put 3,000 passengers on a ship, you need to furnish organized activities to keep everyone happy. **Cruise directors** and **activity coordinators** arrange events for guests to meet one another and have a more enjoyable experience. People who fill these positions generally have outgoing personalities.

These positions require the ability to "break the ice," by encouraging passengers to participate in dancing, karaoke, singles nights, and talent contests. Because cruising is family-oriented, **youth activity coordinators** are hired to organize activities and events for children and adolescents. A close land-based equivalent of a youth activity coordinator would be a camp counselor.

Cruise lines don't overlook their gyms, where **aerobics instructors** and **personal trainers** coordinate passenger exercise with weights, spin classes, and other workouts. On some ships, Tai chi and yoga classes are offered, resulting in openings for instructors in those areas. Some cruise lines seek **golf coaches** to work with passengers in one-on-one lessons.

A large cruise ship needs a medical staff to deal with injuries and illnesses. Cruise lines employ **physicians**, **nurses**, and **physician's assistants**. For physicians, cruise lines look for graduation from an accredited medical school and a medical license. For nurses, requirements generally include a registered nurse license. Physician's assistant credentialing can vary, as it can be a loosely used title.

Cruise lines also employ large housekeeping staffs. This includes **room cleaners**, **laundry workers**, **linen keepers**, and **janitors**. These employees work hard to keep a ship clean and to ensure that passengers get fresh bed sheets, pillow covers, toiletries, and towels. Some cruise lines have turned towel service into an art form, where bath towels are sculpted to resemble cute animals. These jobs involve long workdays and can be situated deep within a ship's lower decks.

# *What Does Someone Need to Get Started?*

What's the name of that poem about going down to the sea in ships? It goes something like this...

> *"I must go down to the seas again,*
> *to the lonely sea and the sky,*
> *And all I ask is a tall ship*
> *and a star to steer her by..."*

The poem is *Sea Fever*, by John Masefield. [28] That's all I ask, *"...a star to steer her by."* Well how about $100 or so to get a Merchant Mariner Credential. And don't forget about another $100 and change for a Transportation Worker Identification Credential ($129.75, effective March 19, 2012 [29]). And if an employer wants you to be STCW-certified, think about shelling out another $1,000 or so for a basic course.

Wow! How did it ever get to be like this? Why, it seems like just yesterday that sailors were being shanghaied out of bars and forced to crew on sailing ships. Well, those good old days are gone, as are the severe labor shortages of the 1800s that created them. Today, it's the other way around, where people line up for jobs. And they accept the fact that they'll pay a few entrance fees at the door to get in.

The Merchant Mariner Document, or MMD, has been around for a long time. It used to be called a Z-Card. It's generally required to work on vessels larger than 100 gross tons. At the time of this writing, the MMD is in the process of being phased out by the Merchant Mariner Credential, or MMC. The origins of STCW, or Standards of Training, Certification and Watchkeeping for Seafarers, date back to 1978 (amended in 1995).

STCW certification is required to work on vessels over 200 gross registered tons domestic tonnage or 500 gross registered tons ITC tonnage, seaward of boundary lines. [30] The Transportation Worker Identification Credential, or TWIC, was mandated by the Maritime Transportation Security Act of 2002. [31]

The old Merchant Mariner Document was in the form of a wallet-sized ID card, slightly larger than a driver license. It included the holder's photo, name, address, and other basic information. The current Merchant Mariner Credential, or MMC, resembles a passport booklet. The process for obtaining a MMC is outlined in several pages of directions, forms, and checklists on the website of the National Maritime Center, at *http://www.uscg.mil/nmc/original.asp*. It advises that candidates must hold or be in the process of obtaining a TWIC.

TWICs are issued through the Transportation Security Administration and are valid for a period of five years. They are required for Coast Guard-credentialed merchant mariners, port facility employees, longshore workers, truck drivers, and other personnel requiring unescorted access to secure areas of maritime facilities and vessels regulated by the Maritime Transportation Security Act of 2002. [32]

Additionally, TWIC holders who escort non-TWIC holders in secure areas of MTSA-regulated vessels, facilities, and

OCS facilities are required to have knowledge of the owner/operator's escorting procedures.

**The industry has experienced profound changes** since September 11, 2001. One of the these has been the introduction of the TWIC, or Transportation Worker Identification Credential. The TWIC is required for personnel entering restricted areas, which can include port facilities and vessels. Another change has been the growth of jobs in the maritime security sector. This includes jobs in the areas of port security, vessel security, marine inspection, and cargo inspection. Concerns about ships carrying radioactive dirty bombs, weapons, explosives, and other contraband have led to increased spending and enhanced programs in major port cities. In the photo above, the container ship *CSAV Rio Puelo* is docked at Port Newark, New Jersey on August 6, 2004 during a scare involving lemons suspected of containing a harmful biological substance. 33

The TWIC contains a fingerprint, which is called a biometric. Employees on foreign flag cruise ships do not generally need to hold TWICs. If you find employment on a cruise ship, there's a good chance it will be registered outside the United States, possibly under the flag of Panama, Bermuda, or The Bahamas.

There are a number of offenses that can disqualify an applicant from obtaining a TWIC. These include conviction of espionage, sedition, treason, terrorism, or conspiracy to commit such crimes. There are other disqualifying offenses, such as transporting hazardous materials or unlawful possession of explosives. 34 The complete list of these offenses is provided on the website of the Transportation Security Administration. The process for obtaining a TWIC is also outlined in detail there, at http://www.tsa.gov.

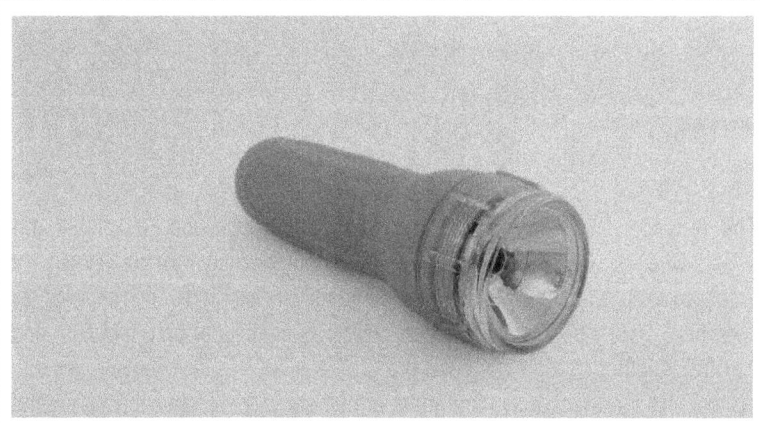

**Of all the personal possessions** one can carry on a commercial vessel, perhaps the most useful is a reliable flashlight. This advice might irrelevant for someone working above deck, but circumstances can change without warning. Crewmembers can be sent below to sound the bilge or get supplies. A fire, generator failure, flooding, or capsize... and someone could find himself plunged into darkness in a chain locker or fish processing compartment two decks below the waterline. A once-familiar ship could turn into a hopeless maze if the lights go out.

STCW establishes industry standards, such as mandatory ten-hour rest periods in any twenty-four hour period for watchkeeping personnel. It requires training in basic first aid, personal survival techniques, firefighting, personal safety, and social responsibility. For applicable persons and vessels, STCW 95 requires an understanding of Automatic Radar Plotting Aids (ARPA), Global Maritime Distress

Safety Systems (GMDSS), and bridge teamwork procedures between a captain and deck officers.

The purpose of STCW is to create uniform competency standards for shipboard personnel throughout the world. In developing STCW, the international maritime community realized that many accidents were attributable to human error. Minimum standards for competency, together with safer operational protocols, were seen as the solution to this problem.

In addition to MMCs, TWICs, and STCW certification, employers may impose their own conditions. These can vary from company to company. Below are some of the requirements for employment with the U.S. Military Sealift Command, the large government employer described earlier in the book. Candidates must:

- be at least 18 years of age.
- be a United States citizen with a valid U.S. passport.
- be capable of speaking, understanding, reading and writing the English language.
- have a Transportation Worker Identification Credential (TWIC) and a valid Merchant Mariner Credential (MMC), issued by the U.S. Coast Guard, and with at least one year of eligibility remaining on it before it is due for renewal.
- be capable of passing an MSC-administered physical examination. Due to often strenuous shipboard duties and extended periods at sea, all applicants must meet MSC medical requirements.
- be drug free and submit to urinanalysis in accordance with the Department of Health and Human Services guidelines.
- be able to obtain and maintain a security clearance. [35]

After people satisfy basic credentialing requirements and start working aboard a vessel, they often become interested in obtaining a Coast Guard license. This is a complex subject, governed by lengthy regulations that address sea time and other requirements to sit for various licenses.

**The U.S. Military Sealift Command,** mentioned on the previous page, operates a large fleet of ships providing logistic support and other services for the U.S. Navy. Its Combat Logistics Force includes replenishment oilers, fast combat support ships, dry cargo-ammunition ships, and an ammunition ship. They provide fuel, food, ordnance, mail, and supplies that enable naval vessels to remain on station for long periods of time. 36 This government employer offers good salaries and benefits for civilian mariners. In the photo above, the *USS New Orleans* receives stores from the *USNS Bridge*.

In general, Coast Guard licenses are divided into two major categories, deck and engine. Deck licenses cover navigation, collision regs (which used to be called rules of the road), seamanship, cargo operations, and related subjects. Engine licenses cover diesel engines, boilers, steam turbines, refrigeration, electricity, evaporators, and related subjects.

One of the reasons why mariner licensing is such a complex subject is because there are many different licenses, and there are sometimes multiple routes available for advancing to a higher license. Licenses range from six-pack operator to unlimited tonnage master, and designated duty engineer to unlimited horsepower chief engineer. That's not even mentioning endorsements, such as towing.

Covering the subject of licensing in a detailed manner would essentially result in duplication of material from the Coast Guard's National Maritime Center. There's no point doing that, since their website covers the subject thoroughly, offering downloadable forms and relevant sections of federal regulations. Therefore, readers who are interested in obtaining a license should visit the National Maritime Center, at http://www.uscg.mil/nmc.

In the meantime, the following pages contain sample questions of the type that have appeared on license exams in the past. ₃₇ As a word of caution, please be advised that the U.S. Coast Guard does not endorse these questions as license exam questions.

### Sample License Questions - General Deck

| 1. You are standing the wheelwatch when you hear the cry, "Man overboard starboard side." You should instinctively _____. |
| --- |
| (a.) give full left rudder |
| (b.) give full right rudder |
| (c.) put the rudder amidships |
| (d.) throw a life ring to mark the spot |

| 2. Your vessel has grounded on a bar. What should you do? |
| --- |
| (a.) If you cannot get clear immediately, lighten the ship by pumping all ballast overboard. |
| (b.) Run the engine full astern to keep from being set further onto the bar. |
| (c.) Switch to the high suction for condenser circulating water, if it is submerged. |
| (d.) All of the above |

3. A crack in the deck plating of a vessel may be temporarily prevented from increasing in length by _____.

(a.) cutting a square notch at each end of the crack

(b.) drilling a hole at each end of the crack

(c.) slot-welding the crack

(d.) welding a doubler over the crack

4. The distance that a ship moves forward with each revolution of its propeller, if there is no slip, is called _____.

(a.) advance          (b.) head reach

(c.) pitch             (d.) transfer

Answers to General Deck Questions 1- 4   (1.) b   (2.) c   (3.) b   (4.) c

## Sample License Questions - General Engine

1. The process of removing moisture from air is known as _____.

(a.) humidification

(b.) dehumidification

(c.) vaporization

(d.) evaporation

2. The rate of heat transfer between the hot and cold fluids passing through a shell-and-tube type heat exchanger will _____.

(a.) remain constant along the tube's length

(b.) be greatest in a single pass counter flow heat exchanger

(c.) remain constant throughout the heat exchanger

(d.) vary from section to section throughout the heat exchanger

3. Coast Guard Regulations (46 CFR) require refrigerated spaces that can be locked from the outside and cannot be opened from the inside to have an audible alarm to sound in _____.

(a.) the chief steward's berthing quarters

(b.) the galley

(c.) the wheelhouse

(d.) a manned location

4. The unlicensed crew list on the Certificate of Inspection reads as follows:3 firemen/watertenders; 3 oilers. The vessel is about to depart on a foreign voyage, and has 3 firemen/watertenders, 2 oilers, and one man, whose MMD is endorsed QMED, any rating. You should _____.

(a.) call the port captain and request another oiler

(b.) sail because your crew requirements are filled

(c.) request a waiver

(d.) check if any of the firemen have enough time for an oiler's endorsement

Answers to General Engine Questions 1 - 4   (1.) b   (2.) d   (3.) d   (4.) b

**Sample License Questions - General Navigation**

1. For navigational purposes, each great circle on the earth has a length of _____.

(a.) 3,600 miles   (b.) 5,400 miles
(c.) 12,500 miles   (d.) 21,600 miles

---

2. What should you apply to a fathometer reading to determine the depth of water?
(a.) Subtract the draft of the vessel.
(b.) Add the draft of the vessel.
(c.) Subtract the seawater correction.
(d.) Add the seawater correction.

---

3. When making landfall at night, the light from a powerful lighthouse may sometimes be seen before the lantern breaks the horizon. This light is called _____.

(a.) diffusion   (b.) backscatter
(c.) loom   (d.) elevation

---

4. Your vessel is leaving New York harbor in dense fog. As the vessel slowly proceeds toward sea, you sight a green can buoy on the starboard bow. Which action should you take?
(a.) Turn hard right to get back into the channel.
(b.) Pass the buoy close to, leaving it to your port.
(c.) Stop and fix your position.
(d.) Stand on, leaving the buoy to your starboard.

## Sample License Questions - Engineering Safety

1. When involved in fighting a fire aboard a ship with an aluminum superstructure, it is important to remember that aluminum structures exposed to the high heat _____.

(a.) generate poisonous fumes

(b.) are more susceptible to collapse than steel structures

(c.) are susceptible to spontaneous ignition

(d.) all of the above

On November 22, 1975, a fire broke out on the cruiser *USS Belknap* after it collided with the aircraft carrier *USS John F. Kennedy* off the coast of Sicily during night operations in the Mediterranean. 38 Top photo shows the *USS Belknap* after the tragic fire. Lower photo shows the *USS Wainwright*, a sister ship of the *USS Belknap*. The design of the *Belknap-class* cruisers was based on a steel hull and aluminum upper works. Aluminum upper works reduce topside weight and improve stability. However, they are vulnerable to fire.

2. Coast Guard Regulations (46 CFR) require that lifejackets shall be _____.

(a.) provided for each person onboard

(b.) provided for all personnel on watch

(c.) readily accessible to persons in the engine room

(d.) all of the above

---

3. When should food or water be provided to survivors after boarding a lifeboat or liferaft?

(a.) after 12 hours

(b.) after 24 hours

(c.) after 48 hours

(d.) Some food and water should be consumed immediately and then not until 48 hours later.

---

4. The preferred method of controlling external bleeding is by _____.

(a.) applying direct pressure on the wound

(b.) elevating the wounded area

(c.) applying pressure on a pressure point

(d.) applying a tourniquet above the wound

---

Answers to Engineering Safety Questions 1 - 4   (1.) b   (2.) d   (3.) b   (4.) a

**Sample License Questions - Collision Regs**

1. INLAND ONLY Your vessel is meeting another vessel head-on. To comply with the rules, you should exchange _____.

(a.) 1 short blast, alter course to the left, and pass stbd to stbd

(b.) 2 short blasts, alter course to the left, and pass stbd to stbd

(c.) 1 short blast, alter course to the right, and pass port to port

(d.) 2 short blasts, alter course to the right, and pass port to port

2. BOTH INTERNATIONAL & INLAND The rules require that a stand-on vessel SHALL take action to avoid collision when she determines that _____.

(a.) risk of collision exists

(b.) the other vessel will cross ahead of her

(c.) the other vessel is not taking appropriate action

(d.) collision cannot be avoided by the give-way vessel's maneuver alone

3. BOTH INTERNATIONAL & INLAND Which is the danger signal?

(a.) A continuous sounding of the fog signal

(b.) Firing a gun every minute

(c.) Five or more short rapid blasts on the whistle

(d.) One prolonged blast on the whistle

4. INLAND ONLY What MAY be used to indicate the presence of a partly submerged object being towed?

(a.) a black cone, apex upward

(b.) two all-round yellow lights at each end of the tow

(c.) the beam of a search light from the towing vessel shown in the direction of the tow

(d.) all of the above

## Sample License Questions - Steam Plants

1. If a ship is to be laid up for an indefinite period, the steam side of the main condenser should be _____.

(a.) filled with moist air

(b.) left under a vacuum

(c.) completely drained of water

(d.) pressurized to approximately 5 psig with nitrogen, 99.5% pure by volume

2. When a turbine bearing shows signs of overheating, you should _____.

(a.) stop the turbine

(b.) immediately reduce speed

(c.) increase the lube oil pump discharge pressure

(d.) increase the cooling water supply to the lube oil cooler

3. Underway on watch in the fireroom, the bridge reports black smoke coming from the stack. This would indicate _____.

(a.) fuel oil temperature too low

(b.) excessive steam atomization pressure

(c.) excessive air-fuel turbulence

(d.) all of the above

4. You are standing a sea watch in the engine room of a steam vessel. To operate at maximum efficiency, adjustments to the boiler combustion control system should be made by setting the _____.

(a.) fuel oil back pressure

(b.) air volume regulators

(c.) fuel/air ratio controller

(d.) forced draft fan damper positions

Answers to Steam Plant Questions 1 - 4  (1.) c  (2.) b  (3.) a  (4.) c

## Sample License Questions - General Safety (Deck)

1. Coast Guard regulations require that all of the following emergencies be covered at the periodic drills on a fishing vessel EXCEPT _____.

(a.) minimizing effects of unintentional flooding

(b.) fire on board

(c.) rescuing an individual from the water

(d.) emergency towing

2. Your ship is sinking rapidly. A container containing an inflatable liferaft has bobbed to the surface upon functioning of the hydrostatic release. Which action should you take?

(a.) Cut the painter line so it will not pull the liferaft container down.

(b.) Swim away from the container so you will not be in danger as it goes down.

(c.) Take no action because the painter will cause the liferaft to inflate and open the container.

(d.) Manually open the container and inflate the liferaft with the hand pump.

3. If, for any reason, it is necessary to abandon ship while far out at sea, it is important that crewmembers should _____.

(a.) separate from each other as this will increase the chances of being rescued

(b.) get away from the area because sharks will be attracted to the vessel

(c.) immediately head for the nearest land

(d.) remain together in the area because rescuers will start searching at the vessel's last known position

4. Your vessel rolls slowly and sluggishly. This indicates that the vessel _____.

(a.) has off-center weights

(b.) is taking on water

(c.) has a greater draft forward than aft

(d.) has poor stability

Answers to General Safety (Deck) Questions 1 - 4  (1.) d   (2.) c   (3.) d   (4.) d

## Sample License Questions - Electricity

1. Ships requiring rapid maneuvering response with a high degree of main propeller shaft control are most often _____.

(a.) steam turbine drive

(b.) direct diesel

(c.) diesel-electric drive

(d.) gas turbine drive

2. The electrician reports to you that he has obtained low (but above 1 megohm) megger readings on the windings of a deck winch motor. Upon checking the records of that motor, you find the readings have consistently been at that level for the last six years. You should, therefore, recommend that the _____.

(a.) motor be replaced

(b.) windings be dried

(c.) windings be cleaned

(d.) readings are acceptable

3. Coast Guard Regulations (46 CFR) state that a continuous trickle charge, supplied from the ship's service power system, is required for batteries supplying power to the _____.

(a.) radios installed in the lifeboats

(b.) portable radios for the lifeboats

(c.) emergency power systems for radar

(d.) emergency gas turbine generator starting system

4. To repair a small electrical motor that has been submerged in saltwater, you should _____.

(a.) wash it with fresh water and apply an external source of heat

(b.) renew the windings

(c.) send it ashore to an approved service facility

(d.) rinse all electrical parts with a carbon tetrachloride cleaning solvent and then blow dry the motor with compressed air

Answers to Electricity Questions 1 - 4  (1.) c   (2.) d   (3.) d   (4.) a

**Sample License Questions - Motor Plants & Auxiliaries**

---

1. A controllable pitch propeller on a diesel driven vessel eliminates the need for _____.

(a.) friction clutches

(b.) disconnect clutches

(c.) reversing gears

(d.) reduction gears

---

2. Fuel is admitted to a diesel engine cylinder through the _____.

(a.) intake valves

(b.) carburetor

(c.) exhaust ports

(d.) injector nozzles

---

3. Why are heavy fuels not usually prone to the problems of microbiological infection?

(a.) Heavy fuels are subjected to better refining processes which prevent the formation of these growths.

(b.) Most heavy fuels contain chemicals which prevent the growth of fungi and bacteria.

(c.) Microbiological infection does not affect marine fuel but rather the personnel who are involved with the handling, storage and purification of the fuel.

(d.) The necessary nutrients that the organisms feed on are in a more complex form and not available for microbial degradation.

4. The purpose of the flywheel is to _____.

(a.) provide energy to operate the engine between power impulses

(b.) neutralize the primary inertia force of the crankshaft

(c.) reduce the shock of starting loads on the main bearings

(d.) prevent the engine from operating at critical speed

Answers to Motor Plants & Auxiliaries Questions 1 - 4 (1.) c  (2.) d  (3.) d  (4.) a

So You Want to Work on a Boat

# *Applying for a Job*

If you ask three different people how to get a job on a commercial vessel, you'll probably get three different answers. Because this is a somewhat unique industry, it's easy for outsiders to speculate that there are special ways to get hired. Some folks believe you need a relative on the inside. Others insist you need to pay money up front. Another favorite is that you have to go through some sort of apprenticeship or internship.

The simple truth is that there isn't much mystery to getting a job on a commercial vessel. Sure, it definitely helps if you know someone. But let's assume that like most people reading this book, you don't have an uncle who's a tugboat captain. You're aunt isn't the recruitment manager for a cruise line. Where's the best place to start?

The most direct route to getting a job is to visit websites of vessel operators and apply for posted positions. Some companies accept resumes directly, while others advise applicants to contact the maritime unions through which they fill their seagoing positions. At the end of the book, commercial vessel operators are listed by industry.

Maritime trade magazines are another good source for job leads. Some companies choose not to post job openings on their websites, opting instead for classified ads. Furthermore, not every company has the time or resources to maintain a web presence. But even companies that maintain websites find that trade magazines are an effective platform for attracting applicants.

Employment websites are another worthwhile resource. However, general purpose employment websites tend to group jobs under commonly searched categories, such as education, engineering, financial, or health. They don't generally contain a *maritime* category. That's because the larger share of their visitor traffic is geared toward non-maritime employment.

The *transportation* section is as close as you'll get to the maritime industry with most general purpose employment websites. General purpose employment websites can offer good leads, if you know how to look for them. This comes down to using search keywords that yield meaningful results. Readers can collect good search keywords from the earlier chapters of this book that describe jobs on inland and ocean-going vessels.

There are numerous websites tailored specifically for the maritime industry. If you conduct a few internet searches for *maritime jobs, tugboat jobs, ferry jobs, jobs on ships,* etc., you'll come across a few of these. These sites can include job listings that don't appear in general purpose employment sites.

Job fairs are another valuable resource. The U.S. Military Sealift Command conducts job fairs throughout the United States. The U.S. Coast Guard and U.S. Army Corps of Engineers also conduct job fairs for civilian employment opportunities. Although job fairs are excellent resources, there aren't a large number of them that focus on the maritime industry. Cruise lines hold recruitment events throughout the world, which reflects the global nature of cruise ship staffing.

After finding something you want to apply for, what's the best way to contact companies? These days, many employers encourage jobseekers to apply for positions online. Some companies provide toll-free job hotlines, or invite applicants to fax resumes. This is to avoid excluding candidates who don't have access to a computer.

**Why do employers use blind ads?** Here's an example of a blind ad: *West Coast yacht club seeks tender operator Memorial Day to Labor Day. USCG launch operator license & one year small vessel experience. Send cover letter and resume to yachtclubtender@hotmail.com.* Blind ads are used by marine transportation companies as well. Here's an example: *East Coast towing company seeks 500 ton captain for relief work. Current STCW. Send cover letter and resume to TMK at P.O. Box 450226, Hampton Roads, Virginia 23320.* With a blind ad, you don't know who you're sending your resume to. People can find themselves applying to their own company if they aren't careful. Employers use blind ads for a number of reasons. They might want to fire someone without alerting the whole world about their intentions. Yacht clubs might use blind ads to avoid being approached by members who want their kids to be hired for summer jobs. This can make club officers uncomfortable in choosing one friend's kid over another's.

However, if you have your way with choices, online is the way to go, since it offers a number of advantages. It's free. It's fast. And since e-mail provides instantaneous confirmation, you can be reasonably confident that a company received your resume. Aside from saving yourself the expense of postage and premium quality paper, applying online is sometimes the only option.

**Why don't I see more job postings for firemen or watertenders?** There was a time when U.S. ships were predominantly steam-powered and European ships were diesel-powered. Steamships often had boilers installed port and starboard, with burner fronts facing each other. The space between boilers was called the fireroom. Here, *firemen* controlled air and fuel flow by operating air registers and oil burners. *Watertenders* monitored steam drum water levels, a crucial duty in preventing boiler explosions. Watertenders regularly checked levels in reserve feed tanks to ensure an adequate supply of boiler feedwater to make up for steam losses and leaks in the system. The fireroom was a tough place to work, with temperatures easily exceeding 120°F in tropical waters. The upper levels of these machinery spaces could be hotter still, near the Ljungstrom air preheaters that warmed incoming air for the boilers. Today, most ships use large low-speed diesel engines. The days of steam as a prime mover are fading into history, along with the asbestos blankets that once hung in firerooms, ready to douse out fuel oil fires.

That's because some employment ads don't offer physical addresses to which applicants can send their resumes. Some websites take it a step further and accept resumes only from registered users. Jobseekers register by creating a username and password in those instances. As with anything involving the Internet, readers are advised to use caution when providing personal information online.

Since everyone doesn't own a computer and internet connection, this can create a hardship for some. One solution is to use libraries or government offices that provide internet access as a public service. However, these entities sometimes limit computer time for visitors. While purchasing a computer could be a financial burden, it can save money in the long run.

A computer can be used to generate personalized cover letters from standard templates. A computer can be used to search for prospective employers on the Internet. It can be used to research companies in preparation for interviews. It can also be used to apply for mariner credentials. There's virtually no argument that can be made for not using a computer and the Internet in this endeavor.

However, there IS one way where an old-fashioned method can sometimes accomplish the best results. That's through the good old channel of personal contacts. News of job openings travels quickly through the grapevine of friends and relatives. Some companies like the idea of filling a vacancy with someone who comes endorsed by a veteran employee.

It can be a way for an organization to reward good workers. For companies that take pride in being family-oriented, hiring someone's kid reinforces that image. It fosters loyalty to the company. It strengthens the team spirit and camaraderie created by company picnics and other events. Hiring an insider also means there's a strong incentive for a parent or sibling to pressure the new hire to perform well.

On the other hand, some companies want fresh candidates from the outside, fearing that old-timers could acquire undue influence over new hires as a reward for getting them a job. Another reason for hiring from the outside is that a company might not want to give the appearance of favoritism among its employees. After all, some people's relatives are going to get hired, while others are not.

Regardless of whether people find job leads through trade magazines, company websites, or family recommendations, they're going to need to compose a good resume, cover letter, and brush up on interviewing skills. Putting your best foot forward here requires writing skills and presentation skills. In a nutshell, the process boils down to how well you can package yourself.

We aren't naturally born with the ability to market ourselves, but it's a skill we can learn. Let's discuss how to effectively use a *resume*, *cover letter*, and *interview* skills to land a good job. Throughout the next few pages, readers will find sample cover letters and resumes. These can be used as templates in developing your own versions.

In today's job market, it's an unfortunate reality that most resumes and cover letters go unanswered. This isn't because companies want to be heartless or rude. Most companies simply don't have the manpower to respond to every resume received. Maritime employers are being swamped by applications from every which way in this difficult economy.

The flood of applicants comes from the experienced as well as the inexperienced. Some jobseekers are veterans with twenty years of experience under their belts. Some are fresh out of school. Some are refugees from areas of the maritime industry that are going through downturns. Whatever the case, the volume of job applications being received by most companies is overwhelming. Therefore, don't take it personally if a company doesn't respond to your resume and cover letter.

**Resume** A resume is somewhat like an autobiography. An autobiography is a literary work about someone's life story. Well, a resume is about someone's *professional* life story.

**A captain or mate who pilots an advanced tug such as *Wendy Moran*** needs to be familiar with special controls in the wheelhouse. That's because the *Wendy Moran* uses z-drives to transmit power from two EMD16-645-E6 engines to a set of azimuthing propellers. This gives the 87' tug tremendous maneuverability. Traditional tugboats use propellers mounted on fixed shafts, where fore and aft thrust is controlled by rudder(s). On a z-drive tug, the entire propeller pod rotates, giving unprecedented control. Built in 2000 by Washburn and Doughty Associates in East Boothbay, Maine, the 166 ton steel tug is operated by Moran Towing Corporation. In the photo above, the tug gently nudges the amphibious assault ship *USS Bataan* (LHD 5) away from its pier at Naval Station Norfolk. 39

Although an autobiography might be hundreds of pages in length, one or two pages will do for well-written resume. Here's another interesting similarity. Just like a good autobiography, a resume should be pleasing to read and must keep a reader's attention.

After a quick read, a busy editor at a publishing house can decide very quickly whether she wants to publish an autobiography or throw it into the garbage. Likewise, after about 20 seconds, a busy personnel manager can decide whether she wants to keep reading a resume, or feed it into a paper shredder.

---

Elizabeth Roebling
654 Fomalhaut Road
Seattle, Washington 98101

March 6, 2012

Ms. Denise Ford
Vice-President of Human Resources
Pacific Cruises, Inc.
1000 Pacific Loop
San Diego, California 92101

Re: Reference:       Vacancy No. PC12-0056
    Position:        Captain: Unlimited Tonnage-Ocean

Dear Ms. Ford:

I'm interested in serving as a captain with Pacific Cruises, Inc. I'm submitting my resume to be considered for this position, referenced in the Pacific Cruises website as Vacancy No. PC12-0056, Captain: Unlimited Tonnage-Ocean.

I currently work as a staff captain with Trident Cruises, operating out of Seattle, Washington. Since graduating from Massachusetts Maritime Academy in 1998, I've held positions of increasing responsibility with several cruise lines. Although I'm satisfied with my current position, I'm interested in working as a captain. This is a goal I have fostered since embarking on a professional mariner career.

I would be pleased to provide any additional information needed to evaluate my application. Thank you.

Sincerely yours,


Elizabeth Roebling

---

**Elizabeth Roebling**
654 Fomalhaut Road
Seattle, Washington 98101
Telephone (206) 222-4444 ■ e-mail: elizr1998@frontier.net

**Education**
Massachusetts Maritime Academy, B.S. Marine Transportation 1998

**Experience**
*Staff Captain 01/08 - Present **Trident Cruises** Seattle, WA* Duties include assisting captain in management of deck operations on 91,000 ton cruise ship *Trident Alaska*. This involves ensuring adherence to human resources policies, supervising deck officers, and carrying out compliance programs for environmental regulations.

*First Officer 01/05 - 12/07 **Trident Cruises** Seattle, WA* Served as watch officer on 72,000 ton cruise ship, *Trident Hawaii*, and 91,000 ton cruise ship, *Trident Alaska*. Developed standard operating procedures for oil spill prevention and response plan. Performed stability calculations.

*Second Officer 03/02 - 12/04; **Third Officer**, 11/01 - 02/02 **Galaxy Cruises International**, Los Angeles, CA* Served as watch officer on 68,000 ton cruise ship, *Galaxy Pride*. Trained crew in celestial and electronic navigation. Conducted drills for passengers.

*Third Officer 12/98 - 10/01 **Ambassador Cruise Line**, Miami, FL* Served as watch officer on 54,000 ton cruise ship, *Ambassador Splendor*. Conducted drills for passengers. Monitored vessel overhaul in Fincantieri Shipyard 04/01 to 06/01.

**Licenses** U.S.C.G. Master, Unlimited Tonnage, Unlimited Ocean

**Certifications** STCW, GDMSS, ARPA, Radar Observer

**Training** 2008 Human Resources Consultants *Avoiding Lawsuits in the Workplace,* 2006 U.S. Merchant Marine Academy *Bridge Simulator Training*

**Puget Sound Youth Center** *Volunteer* Mentoring teens about careers and education

Most resumes never get a second look because there's simply not enough time in the day to review each one in detail. Many are disqualified because they don't even come near the mark. Out of desperation, many people use a shotgun approach to send their resumes everywhere they can. Some applicants don't carefully read the qualifications sections of job postings.

The licensing and credentialing requirements for commercial vessel jobs are essentially non-negotiable. In this respect, boat jobs are not like land-based jobs, where 10 years of supervisory experience might be substituted for a college degree when applying for a manager position. In contrast, if a job requires a 1600 ton mate license, that's all there is to it. Either a person holds the license or she doesn't.

So far as resumes go, there are those that would have had a decent chance, but failed because they were excessively long, poorly written, deceptively written, or confusing. When a resume raises too many questions, it works against an applicant. Seasoned human resources professionals are adept at sniffing out writing styles aimed at hiding things from a prospective employer.

There are also those resumes that hit the bullseye and result in an invitation to an interview. And that's what we want. How does a resume accomplish this? It presents you in an organized and well-written manner. That means no spelling errors and no grammatical errors. It means contact information is correct. Odd as it may seem, there are resumes prepared by highly intelligent people where the contact information is incorrect.

Companies realize that people are human and make mistakes. But if there are too many mistakes that are glaring in nature, forgiveness can be unlikely. Call it principle, or call it old-fashioned values.

Some companies might not give a second chance to a person who doesn't seem to care enough to get it right on a resume. A company might assume that an applicant's work ethic is as sloppy as his grammar skills. That could be an incorrect or unfair assumption, but that's how life works.

It might be annoying to hear that adage, "You never get a second chance to make a good first impression." But it holds true. A minor spelling mistake doesn't mean someone wouldn't be a good activities coordinator on a cruise ship. But since there isn't often enough time for companies to give everyone the benefit of the doubt, small things can undermine an otherwise worthy application.

In being well-organized, a resume must present information in a format that's logical, chronologically correct, pleasing to the eye, and not unnecessarily long. If the information is intelligently arranged, one page can suffice. If there are lots of licenses, endorsements, and certifications, a second page could be necessary. If a resume is seven pages long, something is wrong.

People in human resources aren't going to sift through a seven-page resume to figure out if someone is STCW-certified. They aren't going to start scribbling handwritten notes on the side to try to figure out the date an applicant started with a ferry company or left the company. No one has patience for that these days.

Remember, this is a sales pitch of sorts. Before a company can call you in for an interview, get to like your pleasant personality, or be impressed with your 500 ton captain license, they have to like you on paper. You're selling a product, and that product is you. A good sales pitch has to "hook" the reader relatively quickly and continue making a favorable impression.

---

Matthew Green
222 Estuary Lane
Houma, Louisiana 70361

March 6, 2012

John Harrison
Personnel Manager
Harper Offshore Services
P.O. Box 262
Galliano, Louisiana 70354

Re: Application for QMED

Dear Mr. Harrison:

I am interested in employment as a QMED with Harper Offshore Services. I realize you have no current openings at this time. However, I'm providing my resume after reading your company's invitation to submit resumes for future consideration.

I presently work as a QMED in the inland towing industry. I'm interested in offshore work because I'm seeking opportunities for advancing my career on larger vessels. Presently, I'm studying to become a Designated Duty Engineer, 1,000 HP. I have extensive experience with Cummins and Detroit diesels, as well as large low-speed diesels.

Please feel free to call me if vacancies for QMEDs arise at Harper Offshore Services. Thank you.

Yours truly,

Matthew Green

---

**Matthew Green**
222 Estuary Lane
Houma, Louisiana 70361
Telephone (985) 321-4444  ■  e-mail: greenm1972@calnet.com

**Experience**
*QMED 06/10 - Present **Gulf Barge Lines**, Houma, LA* Duties include operation and maintenance of engine room machinery aboard *Diane Forrester*, a 85' towboat on the Mississippi River. This includes working on Cummins diesels. Responsibilities also include performing repairs on deck gear.

*Wiper 11/09 - 05/10 **Glacier Container Line**, Portland, OR* Stood engine room watches aboard *Ocean Flyer*, a 60,000 ton container ship. Assisted engineering officers in operation of Wärtsilä low-speed diesel engine. Monitored gauges, auxiliary equipment, and electrical systems. Performed maintenance duties, including lubrication, painting, and cleaning.

*Machinist's Mate 2005 - 2009 **United States Navy*** Served aboard *USS Lake Champlain* and other surface vessels. Experience in gas turbine operations, machine shop operations, and welding. Highly familiar with General Electric LM2500 gas turbine plants. Honorable Discharge.

**Education**
• *Distance Learning Institute*, Fall 2004 Completed 12 credits in Mechanical Engineering Technology.
• Alexander Hamilton High School, 2004 General Diploma.

**Certifications**
QMED (Oiler), STCW95, TWIC, Current First-Aid and CPR

**Training**
Currently studying to become Designated Duty Engineer - 1,000 HP, Gulf Barge Lines - Diesel Engine Maintenance, Gulf Barge Lines - Orientation Program

**Activities**
Bread Basket Food Bank - Volunteer

Is there a standard format that's acceptable? A resume is a professional summary. Although it may contain individual choices in sentence structure or writing style, good resumes tend to follow standard formats.

**Leaving a clean wake** The advent of the position of *cruise ship environmental officer* reflects the importance of environmental compliance on the high seas. This position, described in the chapter about jobs on ocean-going vessels, symbolizes good environmental stewardship. It also demonstrates a company's due diligence in executing regulatory compliance programs. Oil spills, chemical spills, and other discharges are commonly treated as crimes nowadays. This means shipboard officers and company executives can be prosecuted in criminal court and face the possibility of imprisonment. And it doesn't necessarily take a catastrophic oil spill to result in criminal charges. Sometimes things of an administrative nature can lead to criminal prosecution, such as failing to maintain proper documentation for oily waste or ballast water management programs.

After all, how many acceptable ways are there to present a summary of one's training, education, military service, licenses, work experience, and professional memberships? Despite small differences in editorial style or layout, most good resumes are similar in the way they present this information.

A good rule of thumb is to place contact information at the top of the page, in a centered format. Contact information should include an applicant's name, address, and telephone number. Deciding whether to include a home number or a cell phone number is a personal call. Including a home number shows an employer that an applicant is legitimately located at a bona fide residence.

However, if someone knows he won't be home to pick up the phone, it could be a good idea to additionally include a cell phone number. If you have an e-mail, include it. It's best to use e-mail addresses that aren't too personal. It could be fun to use amusing e-mail addresses with friends. But when it comes to employers, basic e-mail addresses made up of names or initials are safe bets.

The next section in a resume could list an applicant's education. Some people instead choose to list work experience first. Either format is okay. Whichever format you use, list the most recent education or work experience at the top and work your way down. For college, list the school, degree, major, and year of graduation. For high school, list the school, type of diploma, and year of graduation.

Some experts say you don't need to include the year of graduation because doing so reveals your age and can result in age discrimination. That's always a possibility. Without getting into the legal issues about disclosure of information in a resume, think of it this way. People who provide an honest summary of work experience reveal their age anyway. In listing work experience, you could use bullets or dots to separate paragraphs.

Write summaries of your work experience in a clear, concise, and direct style. For instance, this is good: **Dockmaster** *May 2010 to September 2010 - Supervised two* *tender operators and one gas dock attendant at Ferry Point Marina. Collected fees from boat owners using overnight slips. Performed maintenance and repairs on 23' diesel tender. Responsible for tracking revenues and inventories of concession stand.*

**This is a global industry, which means it's a global job market.** Many of the oil tankers, chemical tankers, and LNG tankers out there are operated by corporations based in every corner of the globe. *Norman Lady* is an LNG tanker, meaning it transports liquefied natural gas. LNG is a vapor at normal atmospheric conditions. However, it is transported in a liquid state by reducing its temperature. *Norman Lady* has a cargo capacity of 87,600 cubic meters. It was delivered in 1973 and is owned by Methane Carriers Ltd, with Höegh LNG Fleet Management serving as the technical manager. The 71,469 ton ship is powered by a General Electric-Kvaerner Brug plant that gives it a speed of 18 knots. 40 *Norman Lady* and the attack submarine *USS Oklahoma City* were involved in a collision east of the Strait of Gibraltar on November 13, 2002. Fortunately, no one was hurt on either vessel, although the submarine suffered damage to its periscope and sail. 41

That's direct and straightforward, and preferable to something like this: ***Dockmaster** Summer 2010 - I was employed in a managerial capacity at Ferry Point Marina, which involved using strong organizational skills to oversee various waterfront activities.* The first passage is clear and direct. It states what you did. The second passage is somewhat vague.

Be thorough in providing start and end dates with employers. If a resume shows gaps in employment, think about how to explain them to avoid creating a negative impression. Employers realize it isn't easy out there. They know that folks are having a tough time. It isn't a crime to be out of work for a couple of months, half a year, or even longer.

But if that's the case, be prepared to explain what you did during those time periods. Employers aren't afraid of people who were out of work. But they are wary of gaps that might suggest a drug problem or other personal issues. In listing military service, include the branch of service, years served, rank at time of discharge, and type of discharge.

Just as with education, list professional licenses in reverse chronological order, starting with the most recent license at the top. Don't forget to include endorsements. And don't overlook training and certifications, such as STCW, Radar Observer, or a supervisory skills course. If you have a MMC and TWIC, include those things.

If an employer sees you've completed STCW and mariner credentialing requirements, that means they'll save money in hiring you over someone who has to jump through hoops to satisfy those things. Additionally, it makes you a sure bet. There's no guarantee that everyone who applies for a MMC or TWIC will get one.

As for mentioning hobbies, activities, and clubs, it's up to you. Some experts feel there's no need to go there, and that those things can sometimes be harmful. Others say those things give an employer a better idea of the type of person their prospective candidate is. It's a personal call.

Remember that a resume is a place to list all your attributes. It's good to be polite in life, but don't be shy on a resume. You're doing a little bragging, but you're doing it in a professional manner. A resume is your chance at having a busy personnel manager notice you. You want her to think, "I like this candidate. I'm willing to invest 20 minutes of my busy day to call him in for an interview."

**Tell me a little bit about yourself.** A job **interview** is your chance to make a company want to hire you. From this discussion, it seemed like the resume was supposed to do that. Well, both are equally important. A resume outlines your qualifications. It shows your basic eligibility for a job. It gets an employer interested in meeting with you to learn more. But the interview is personal. A resume is an initial sales pitch for a product, the product being you. And the interview is a demonstration of that product in front of the prospective buyer.

Think of it this way. To get to this point, you did lots of legwork. You scoured classified ads. You researched lots of companies. You combed the Internet until your eyes became glazed from staring at a computer screen. You polished your resume until it was perfect. You took the time to draft personalized cover letters. Now use the interview to bring everything together.

Remain confident throughout the interview by telling yourself that you're sitting in that chair because the company is seriously interested in hiring you. Human resources departments are busy. They don't call people in to chat over coffee. They want to find good employees without wasting inordinate amounts of time doing so.

But they want to inspect the goods. This means you'll be closely observed in how well you answer questions, how well you communicate, how you make eye contact, how you conduct yourself physically, and how you dress. It's a test of sorts. There are no grades. It's a pass or fail test.

It's always good to get to an interview with time to spare. That's why leaving the house a few minutes early is a good idea, so that a delay at a railroad crossing doesn't turn into a crisis. While everyone knows that, it's also important not to arrive too early. A company doesn't want someone sitting in their reception area for 45 minutes waiting for an interview.

It's important to dress accordingly. That doesn't mean going out and getting fitted for a $700 custom suit. But no one ever hurt themselves by wearing a nice conservative outfit to an office interview. Keep in mind that you could get called in to interview aboard a vessel, where showing up overdressed could be as awkward as not dressing businesslike enough.

When you're sitting in the hot seat, be confident and polite. Be prepared for more than one round of interviews. You may initially meet with a personnel manager. You may then be taken to meet one of the company's captains or operations superintendents. It's important to make eye contact throughout the process. Try to smile when you greet your interviewer. Give a firm handshake.

Perhaps the most important part of the interview is preparation. An interview might last only 20 minutes. But a smart applicant will conduct meaningful research before showing up. This means learning what the position involves. Most company websites provide information about their history, their fleet, their management team, their operations, and corporate philosophy. This is required reading.

Keep in mind that an interview can go beyond just technical questions about your background and qualifications. Sure, you should be prepared to discuss your education, training, and experience. Be prepared to discuss how you came to be interested in the maritime industry. Be prepared to discuss your opinion on the pros and cons of electronic charts, the nuts and bolts of your experience with EMD powertrains, or the most valuable thing you learned in bridge simulator training.

But be prepared to answer trickier questions that could require some preparation. These include questions along the lines of:

"Why should we hire you?"

"Why do you want to work for us?"

"What would you consider to be your biggest weakness?"

"Why did you leave your last employer?"

"Where do you see yourself in this company in two years?"

And an all time favorite of interviewers is, "Tell me about yourself."

Some questions can be open-ended, like that last one. In answering them, be straightforward and direct. Sometimes a seasoned interviewer already knows the answer to a question he's asking. He just wants to see how you answer. Be positive when you discuss your former employer or supervisor. Make it clear that you're interested in the position at hand. Let the interviewer know you're willing to study whatever you need to learn before coming aboard. Be gracious and thank the interviewer for calling you in.

The **cover letter** is the easiest part of this effort. It's difficult to put together a good resume. You might have to figure out an intelligent way to condense years of experience into a few short paragraphs. And it's difficult to prepare for an interview. It could take days of rehearsing to feel confident for the big day. But cover letters are a snap in comparison. They're the easiest part of the equation to get right.

It's important to remember the purpose of a cover letter, which is to introduce yourself and your resume. A good cover letter is about three paragraphs long. It should begin with a personal salutation, such as *Dear Ms. Adams*. If you aren't able to learn the name of the person to whom you're directing the letter, use *Dear Madam or Sir*. The first paragraph should express your interest in the position. It should identify the job title. It shouldn't be difficult to insert people's names, company names, and job titles into a standard cover letter template on a computer.

After expressing your interest in a position, let the cover letter state why you feel you're a good candidate. Describe your work experience, training, and education. Tie this together with the job description and duties. Explain why your particular skills would enable you to carry out the duties of the job. But don't go into to excessive detail. That's the job of the resume.

If you're applying for a deckhand job, mention the fact that you served as a deckhand on a commuter ferry for two years. Mention things that show you can step into the job without too much hand-holding. It isn't necessary to list every training course you've ever attended. Leave that for the resume.

Some people like to include a career objective in a cover letter or resume. That's a personal choice. It can show that an applicant has ambition. It can show direction and motivation. However, it can sometimes obscure things.

Sometimes the "extra luggage" of such information can get in the way of the primary message, which is why you want the job at hand and why you'd be a good fit for it. Also, *too much information* can sometimes be harmful.

Let's say you're applying for the position of captain on a commuter ferry. Your cover letter goes on about how you eventually wish to become manager in a maritime company's operations department. Although everyone likes a candidate with goals, someone on the hiring panel might think, "This person is going to want my job in two years!"

Finally, make sure you provide correct contact information on the cover letter, and that the information is consistent with the contact information on your resume. The sample cover letters and resumes in this section should provide some guidance in developing your own.

For good measure, several additional samples are included in the next few pages. Remember that these are provided as guidance. People can tailor their cover letters and resumes to their personal liking, in terms of layout, font selection, borders, shading, and other stylistic attributes.

# Additional cover letters and resumes

John McPherson
125 Pilothouse Terrace
Capstan, New Jersey 11132

February 10, 2012

Ms. Helen Smith
Manager of Human Resources
Yankee Clipper Ferry Company
117 Gyrocompass Drive
Cutty Sark, New York 10003

Re: Application for Deckhand Position - Posting No. 04034

Dear Ms. Smith:

I am interested in the deckhand position posted on your company's website. I feel I would be a good candidate for this job because I've worked as a deckhand for three years and have extensive experience in vessel operations.

I presently work as a deckhand for the Thermopylae Water Taxi Company, which operates out of Astoria, Queens. In this capacity, I handle lines, direct passenger traffic, and assist the captain with other duties. I am STCW-certified and hold a TWIC.

I have enclosed my resume. If you wish to reach me during daytime hours, my cell telephone number is (123) 456-7890. I can also be reached via e-mail, at jmcpher@seamail.net. Thank you.

Yours truly,

John McPherson

**John McPherson**
125 Pilothouse Terrace
Capstan, New Jersey 11132
Tel (201)123-4567 ■ jmcpher@seamail.net ■ Cell (123) 456-7890


**Objective**       To earn a 100 ton captain license and command an inland waterway vessel

**Education**       St. Bart Community College - currently pursuing Associate Degree in Business - completed 22 credits. 2007 St. Thomas High School - Academic Diploma

**Experience**      *Deckhand - Thermopylae Water Taxi Company* Astoria, New York - *April 2009 to Present* Duties consist of handling lines in docking vessels, supervising movement of embarking and disembarking passengers, assisting in the maintenance of vessels, and fueling vessels.

*Launch Operator - Fort Lauderdale Boat Basin* *September 2007 to March 2009* Duties consisted of operating 22 foot diesel tender in carrying members and guests to their boats. Duties also included performing maintenance, checking moorings, and issuing guest permits to visiting boats.

*Food Service Assistant Manager - The Bagel & Sandwich Masters 2006 to 2007* Part-time employment during junior and senior years of high school. Duties consisted of preparing customer orders, maintaining inventories of supplies, monitoring employee time cards, and assisting with closing store on a daily basis.

**Licenses**        U.S.C.G. Launch Operator License
**& Training**      STCW, TWIC

Annette Pearson
245 Poplar Court
Augusta, Maine 04330

December 22, 2011

Virginia Fernandez
Superintendent of Marine Operations
Binson Chemical Tankers
25 Ammonia Drive
Groton, Connecticut 06340

Re:   Port Engineer - Posting BCT2012-0089

Dear Ms. Fernandez:

I'm interested in serving as Port Engineer for Binson Chemical Tankers. I currently work in the United States Military Sealift Command as a Second Assistant Engineer. I have held engineering positions on commercial vessels since 2005.

I would like to be considered for this position because I have extensive experience in marine diesels, having worked with Burmeister & Wain, General Electric, and Fairbanks Morse plants. I have experience in supervision and understand the importance of preventive maintenance programs in fleet management.

I have attached a resume and a completed application form. Please feel free to call me if you would like to schedule an interview. Thank you.

Yours truly,


Annette Pearson

**Annette Pearson**
245 Poplar Court
Augusta, Maine 04330
Telephone (207) 111-7711 ■ e-mail: annette981@newmail.com

**Education**
*Ocean Mariner's Union Global Training Institute* 2008 Completed studies in diesel engines, boilers, refrigeration, electrical systems, and firefighting. *Maine Department of Education*, GED 2003

**Experience**
*2$^{nd}$ Assistant Engineer 10/11 - Present United States Military Sealift Command* Currently serving aboard dry cargo/ammunition ship *USNS Amelia Earhart,* where duties include standing engine room watches. Overseeing the operation of a Burmeister & Wain diesel plant and auxiliaries. Supervising non-licensed engine room personnel in their watchstanding duties.

*3$^{rd}$ Assistant Engineer 07/08 - 07/11 National Oceanic and Atmospheric Administration* Served aboard research vessels. Oversaw the operation of General Electric diesel-electric plants and auxiliaries. Assisted chief engineer in troubleshooting electrical problems. Helped develop training manual for electrical systems.

*QMED 07/05 - 06/08 National Electric Power & Light* Served as qualified member of the engineering department on towboats transporting coal barges for electric generating stations. Acquired experience with Fairbanks Morse powertrains. Assisted company port engineer and yard superintendent during major overhauls.

*Automotive Associate 07/03 - 06/05 Speedy Lube* Performed automotive maintenance tasks for car owners. This included oil changes and transmission fluid changes.

**Licenses** U.S.C.G. 2$^{nd}$ Asst. Engineer, Unlimited Horsepower, Motor

**Certifications** STCW, TWIC

**Memberships** *Kennebec River Maritime Historical Society* Currently assisting in the restoration of a 1920s era steam launch.

Anton Khrushchev
54 Hemingway Drive
Key West, Florida 33040

January 6, 2012

Captain Steven Hayes
Placement Coordinator
Yacht Staffing Solutions
2212 Coral Avenue
Fort Lauderdale, Florida 33301

Re: Placement as Captain or Mate

Dear Captain Hayes:

I was referred to you by Chief Engineer Kenneth Reyes. Kenneth and I worked together for a few years on the yacht *Valkyrie*. I'm interested in finding employment on a yacht operating on the U.S. East Coast. I currently serve as mate aboard *Zephyr*, a 75' yacht. However, the owner is relocating to the Mediterranean.

Therefore, I would like to find a position on a similar sized vessel. I have extensive experience in vessel operations and would like to continue applying my skills on yachts operating in the Western Atlantic, including The Bahamas, Bermuda, and the Caribbean.

I have enclosed my resume. Please feel to call me. Thank you.

Sincerely yours,

Anton Khrushchev

**Anton Khrushchev**
54 Hemingway Drive
Key West, Florida 33040
Telephone (305) 444-6543 ■ *e-mail: captanton@clipper.net*

**Experience**
***Mate*** *02/07 to present* Duties include sharing piloting duties with captain in the operation of *Zephyr*, a 75' custom-built yacht. I assist in the supervision of a deckhand and stewardess, prepare work orders for shipyard maintenance, review contracts for supplies, and periodically train crewmembers in fire safety and first aid.

***Deckhand*** *03/04 to 02/07* Duties included line handling, engine maintenance, cleaning, painting, and transporting provisions for *Valkyrie*, a 125' Feadship yacht.

***Fire Department Captain*** *(retired)* Served on Bueller County Fire Department (Illinois) from 1984 to 2004. Held rank of Captain from 1997 to 2004, Lieutenant from 1992 to 1997, and Firefighter from 1984 to 1992. BCFD is a municipal fire department serving the community in fire response, emergency response, and hazardous material spill response.

**Education**
Adlai Stevenson High School, Lincolnshire, Illinois 1984 - Academic Diploma

**Licenses**
U.S.C.G. 100 Ton Captain License

**Certifications**
STCW95, Emergency Medical Technician, PADI-Certified Open Water Scuba Instructor

**Training**
Maritime Distance Education - Home Study Course - 100 Ton License
Advanced Firefighting School - Bueller County Fire Department
Leadership Training - Bueller County Office of Human Resources
Hazardous Waste Fires - HAZMAT Solutions, Inc.

# *Training and Education*

We've all heard of that adventurous friend who spent some time working on tugboats during a summer off from college in the 1970s. Or maybe it was a wild and crazy uncle who rode down to Gulfport, Mississippi and signed up on the first commercial vessel he saw after selling his motorcycle and guitar outside a bar. Well, things don't really work like that any more. The world is a different place today.

The industry has become highly regulated. Maritime security has become strict, requiring security checks and Transportation Worker Identification Credentials to enter waterfront facilities. Just as adventure seekers no longer ride around the country by sneaking aboard empty boxcars in railway yards, people don't find commercial mariner jobs by poking around loading docks. Sure, there are exceptions. A cook could get hired over a couple of beers at a local bar. A deckhand could be signed up on the spot by a fishing boat captain whose trawler is shorthanded for a trip. But in general, the industry runs by strict protocols and exacting professional standards.

That's why training and education are important for people who want to advance their careers. Yes, there are entry-level positions for which an applicant needs nothing more than a strong back, a pair of work gloves, and a willingness to work hard. But as with any industry, training and education open doors to better opportunities.

Training commercial mariners is a multimillion dollar business in itself. Schools include maritime academies, specialized colleges, training institutes, and license prep companies. There are training centers with sophisticated bridge simulators that offer ARPA (automatic radar plotting aid) and advanced piloting courses, and there are training centers with a handful of desks and chairs that teach boating safety and six-pack license courses.

**Don't throw your sextants overboard just yet.** Back in the 1990s, the U.S. Naval Academy made some changes in the way midshipmen used sextants in their celestial navigation training. This raised concerns in some circles that sextants would be eliminated from the curriculum. However, the Academy was not planning to do away with sextants. They were only planning to change the way in which midshipmen used information obtained from them. Instead of carrying out a laborious 22-step mathematical calculation, midshipmen would enter information into a computer program. 42 Some tech-savvy mariners see sextants as historical artifacts from the days of coal-burning ships. But if a war or other apocalyptic event ever disabled the satellites that provide data to GPS receivers, those same people would view the sextant very differently.

Selecting a facility depends on a person's needs, ambitions, budget, and schedule. There's a commonly used saying that goes, "You get what you pay for." Perhaps an apt expression for selecting maritime training would be, "Pay for what you need and want."

Maritime academies offer four-year programs leading to bachelor degrees in marine transportation, marine engineering, naval architecture, and other majors geared toward the maritime industry. The academies incorporate courses into their curricula to prepare students for the unlimited tonnage third mate or unlimited horsepower third assistant engineer license exams.

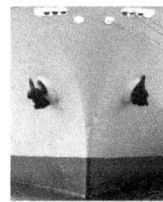 **Going up the hawsepipe** The large tunnel at the front of a ship through which the anchor chain passes is called the hawsepipe. "Going up the hawsepipe" is an expression for the process of starting at an entry-level position, such as ordinary seaman, and working your way to licensed officer, as opposed to going to a maritime school.

Academies generally operate under a regimental system where students are called cadets. Cadets wear uniforms and follow a strict class structure in which upper classmen supervise lower classmen. As part of their education, cadets go to sea for a few months a year and operate an academy training ship. In addition to providing shipboard training, the cruises provide the necessary sea time to sit for license exams. The U.S. Merchant Marine Academy uses a slightly different system, where midshipmen are assigned to commercial vessels during their second and third years of studies. [43]

There are community colleges and four-year colleges which offer other types of programs for working in the maritime industry, such as inland vessel operations and shipbuilding. There are training institutes whose curricula are geared toward license preparation and professional certifications. The courses may cover STCW subjects, diesel engine operations, electronic charts, or radar certification. Training institutes usually dispense with elective courses that aren't directly relevant to vessel operations.

**Thinking beyond the license** Commercial mariners tend to be practical when exploring the subject of training and education. In other words, "What do I need to learn to get my license?" That's understandable, but the learning process doesn't necessarily end there. Maritime education is a vast body of knowledge that can open doors to endless options. Learning about intermodal freight transport can open doors to job opportunities in container terminals. Taking classes in marine insurance can set the foundation for a career in claims processing. Learning about maritime security can provide the inspiration for entering a very dynamic sector of the industry, which covers issues that range from assessing piracy threats on international waters to safeguarding critical cargo operations in LNG terminals. In the photo above, the LNG carrier *Berge Boston* is assisted by the tugs *Harold Reinauer II* and *Freedom* in Boston, Massachusetts. 44 The compelling security issues that arise in LNG transport are self-evident.

There are self-study programs where students can buy books and CDs and pace themselves for license preparation. Choosing a program is largely a matter of personal and economic factors that include a person's age, family situation, and tuition budget.

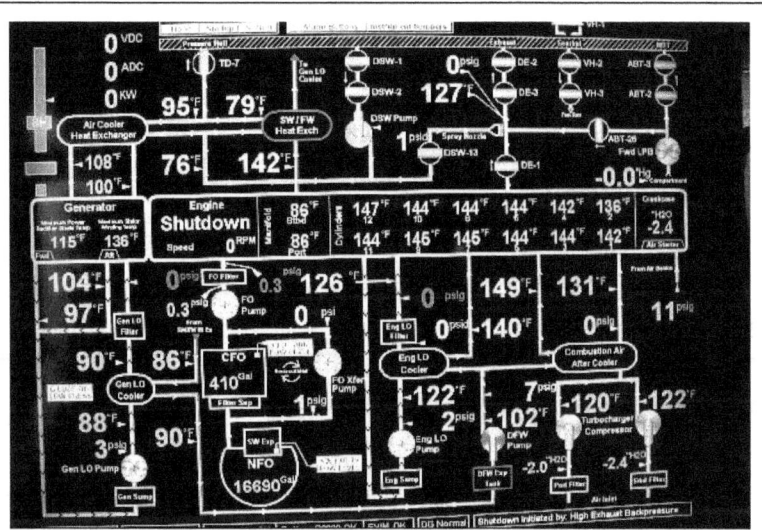

**A most universal skill** Whether someone is a chief engineer with ten years of sea time or a deckhand with ten days on the job, one particular skill is very valuable today. And most readers possess this skill without even giving it a second thought. This is the ability to use computers. Virtually everything on a modern vessel works with computers. Navigation is handled with electronic charts. Cargo operations are performed at computer terminals in tanker pumprooms. Engine room personnel monitor diesel engines from computer consoles that summarize vital operating parameters. The LCD display above shows temperatures, pressures, and other important information for a Caterpillar 3512B V12 generator. In addition to their application in deck, engine, and cargo operations, computers are an important shipboard administrative tool. They help keep track of time cards, spare parts inventories, and correspondence.

An eighteen-year-old can enjoy many options in terms of full-time programs. But someone who's thirty-something with a couple of kids wouldn't necessarily have that kind of freedom. The older candidate might need to figure out ways to juggle babysitting, grocery shopping, household chores, and a full-time job with attending classes, doing homework, and studying for exams.

Choosing the right educational institution also depends on what a person wants to walk away with. If someone wants a third mate license together with a college degree in marine transportation or international trade, a four-year degree program at an academy is a logical choice.

If someone wants a marine engineer's license but isn't opting for a college degree, there are other options, such as training centers, self-study programs, and professional mariner programs (sometimes offered at the academies themselves). Some people want to learn about diesel engines, refrigeration plants, and marine electrical systems, but don't want to take the calculus and physics courses required to earn a degree in engineering.

The pages ahead describe schools that offer maritime education and training. These include maritime academies, maritime union training schools, colleges, and other entities. This book doesn't recommend or endorse any one institution over another. The advantages or disadvantages of selecting one type of school over another can depend upon a person's individual needs.

Readers should conduct research on their own to learn about tuition, courses offered, flexibility of attendance, and accreditation. Some union schools are geared toward providing courses for their membership, while others serve the public at large. Check with the schools themselves to learn about admissions and eligibility requirements. Schools are listed in alphabetical order.

The **Calhoun MEBA Engineering School** is a private facility located in Easton, Maryland. It provides training for members of the Marine Engineers' Beneficial Association and other maritime industry professionals. The School offers courses in engine and deck subjects. Engine courses include diesel engineering, gas turbine engineering, steam engineering, refrigeration, welding, and other subjects. Deck courses include advanced cargo operations, advanced shiphandling, automatic radar plotting aids, bridge resource management, and other subjects. [45] For more information, visit http://mebaschool.org.

**California Maritime Academy** is located in Vallejo, California and is part of the California State University system. The Academy offers degrees in mechanical engineering, business administration, international business & logistics, global studies & maritime affairs, marine transportation, and other majors. Aboard the training ship *Golden Bear,* students complement their shoreside education with shipboard training. Students are designated as cadets and participate in regimental activities. Qualified students can take the U.S.C.G. third mate unlimited tonnage or third assistant engineer unlimited horsepower license exams. The Academy's Extended Learning Program offers courses in bridge resource management, radar training, STCW, and other subjects. For more information, visit www.csum.edu. [46]

**Fletcher Technical Community College**, located in Houma, Louisiana, serves students with two programs, Marine Operations and Integrated Production Technologies. The Marine Operations Program covers marine safety, seamanship, navigation, and related subjects. The Integrated Production Technologies program is geared toward oil and natural gas production and covers instrumentation, process systems, computer applications, and related subjects. For more information, visit www.ftcc.edu. [47]

**Great Lakes Maritime Academy** was founded in 1969 and is part of Northwestern Michigan College. Located in Traverse City, Michigan, the Academy offers degree programs in business administration and applied science.

Qualified students can sit for the U.S.C.G. third mate unlimited tonnage and first class Great Lakes pilot, or third assistant engineer unlimited horsepower license exams. The Academy has a 224' training ship named *State of Michigan*. It was formerly the *Persistent*, a Stalwart-class submarine surveillance vessel. Visit https://www.nmc.edu/maritime for more information. 48

**Kingsborough Community College - Maritime Technology Program** This college is part of the City University of New York, or CUNY, and offers a program where students can earn an associate degree in maritime technology. The campus is located in Brooklyn, near the approaches to New York Harbor. The two-year program is 60 credits and covers coursework in vessel operations, coastal piloting, vessel technology, propulsion systems, marine electronics, and related subjects. For more information, visit www.kbcc.cuny.edu. 49

**Maine Maritime Academy** is a public college located in Castine, Maine. There is a regimental system which is required for some majors and optional for others. The Academy offers associate degree, bachelor degree, and masters degree programs. Majors include marine engineering operations, marine engineering technology, marine transportation operations, international business & logistics, and other subjects. The training ship *State of Maine* serves as a seagoing lab and classroom, providing "hands-on" training for students to learn shipboard operations. Qualified students can sit for the U.S.C.G. third mate unlimited tonnage or third assistant engineer unlimited horsepower license exams. For more information, visit www.mainemaritime.edu. 50

**Maritime Institute of Technology and Graduate Studies: Pacific Maritime Institute** is also known as MITAGS:PMI. It provides maritime training for newcomers and experienced commercial mariners. MITAGS:PMI operates in a non-profit capacity and offers several programs, including an AB to Mate Program, Chief Mate/Master Program, as well as tug and barge, state pilot, and other courses. MITAGS is located in Linthicum Heights, Maryland and PMI is located in Seattle, Washington. Coursework covers COLREGs, azipod shiphandling, advanced meteorology, bridge resource management, and other subjects. They also offer a Workboat Mate Program, which consists of classroom simulator and onboard training. Visit http://mitags-pmi.org for more information. 51

**Massachusetts Maritime Academy** is located on Cape Cod, Massachusetts and combines a regimental system with a four-year undergraduate program. The 540' training ship *Enterprise* provides seagoing training. The Academy offers degrees in marine engineering, marine transportation, marine safety, environmental protection, and other majors. Qualified students can sit for the U.S.C.G. third mate unlimited tonnage or third assistant engineer unlimited horsepower license exams. The Academy's Center for Maritime Training provides resources for professional mariners, covering STCW and other areas. In the Advanced Shiphandling in Manned Models Program, students can operate scale models of large vessels. For more information, visit www.maritime.edu. 52

**Mountwest Community and Technical College** Founded in 1975, Mountwest Community and Technical College is located in Huntington, West Virginia and includes the Inland Waterways Academy Program. The curriculum offers courses in deckhand basic training, ship construction, steersman (Western Rivers), apprentice mate/steersman (inland), and additional subjects. For more information, visit www.mctc.edu. 53

**Paul Hall Center for Maritime Training and Education**
This facility was founded in 1967 and is affiliated with the Seafarers International Union. Located in Piney Point, Maryland, the Center offers courses for deck and engine personnel covering radar, navigation, cargo handling, steam plant operations, motor plant operations, refrigeration, firefighting, shipboard sanitation, welding, galley operations, and other subjects. Some of the features of the campus include the Joseph Sacco Fire Fighting and Safety School, Seafarers Harry Lundeberg School of Seamanship, and Thomas B. Crowley Sr. Education Center. For more information, visit www.seafarers.org. [54]

**Seamen's Church Institute** Training programs at the Seamen's Church Institute date back to 1899. At one time, the Institute ran classes on the rooftop of 25 State Street. During World War II, the Institute trained over 25,000 mariners. Eventually, it came to be known as the Center for Maritime Education (CME), which includes teaching facilities in Paducah, Kentucky and Houston, Texas. The Center's programs include simulator training that covers a multitude of operational scenarios. For more information, visit http://seamenschurch.org. [55]

**Seattle Maritime Academy** is part of Seattle Central Community College. Located in Seattle, Washington, the Academy offers students a Marine Deck Technology Program and a Marine Engineering Technology Program. The deck program concentrates on navigational skills, seamanship, vessel handling, and deck equipment. It is aimed at providing students with the skills to qualify as able seaman. After completing the program, students participate in a 30-day internship aboard a large commercial vessel. The Marine Engineering Technology Program is geared toward marine propulsion plants and auxiliary equipment. Students participate in a 60-day internship aboard a large commercial vessel. For more information, visit http://seattlecentral.edu/maritime. [56]

**Star Center** is a not-for-profit maritime training school in Toledo, Ohio. It was opened in 1983 and expanded to Dania Beach, Florida in 1986. The Center provides license training and STCW certification. Some of its equipment includes a 360° full mission bridge simulator, low-speed diesel engine room simulator, and liquid cargo simulator. Courses include celestial navigation, advanced meteorology, gas turbines, radar recertification, and Military Sealift Command's small arms training. For more information, visit http://star-center.com. [57]

**SUNY Maritime College** is located at Fort Schuyler, in Throgs Neck, New York. It is part of the State University of New York (SUNY). The College offers four-year degrees in marine business & commerce, international transportation & trade, naval architecture, marine engineering, electrical engineering, and other majors. The College offers a M.S. Degree Program in International Transportation Management in its Graduate School. Qualified students can sit for U.S.C.G. third mate unlimited tonnage or third assistant engineer unlimited horsepower license exams. The College is home to the *Empire State VI*, a 565' steam-driven training ship. The College also operates the Department of Professional Education and Training, which offers continuing education programs and other resources for maritime professionals. For more information, visit www.sunymaritime.edu. [58]

**Texas Maritime Academy** is part of Texas A & M University. It is located on Pelican Island in Galveston, Texas and offers four-year degree programs combined with studies aboard the training ship *Texas Clipper*, where students learn the skills to operate commercial vessels. Qualified students can sit for the U.S.C.G. third mate unlimited tonnage or third assistant engineer unlimited horsepower license exams. Undergraduate majors include marine biology, marine sciences, marine transportation, and marine engineering technology. Graduate programs are also offered. For more information, visit www.tamug.edu. 59

**Many training facilities** have addressed the important issue of transitioning to electronic charts. An ECDIS, or Electronic Chart Display and Information System, offers advantages over traditional paper charts, such as the ability to update charts at sea. Also, a navigator can zoom in or out of an electronic chart without having to deal with a large spread of paper. However, using electronic charts is more than merely a matter of convenience for commercial mariners. The International Maritime Organization, or IMO, has introduced timetables making it mandatory to adopt electronic charts. The goal is to bring uniformity to the industry, with deck personnel throughout the world having the same chart reading abilities. This is yet one more example of how commercial mariners will be required to embrace ever-increasingly sophisticated technologies in the future.

**United States Merchant Marine Academy** Located at Kings Point, New York, the Academy is operated under the U.S. Maritime Administration (MARAD), and is one of the nation's five service academies. It was dedicated in 1943 and provides degree programs in marine transportation, maritime operations and technology, marine engineering, and other majors. Qualified students can sit for the U.S.C.G. third mate unlimited tonnage or third assistant engineer unlimited horsepower license exams. Students are called midshipmen and earn their qualifying sea time by sailing on commercial vessels during enrollment at the Academy. For more information, visit http://usmma.edu. [60]

In addition to the educational institutions covered here, there are many privately operated schools that provide quality training in a broad range of license and continuing education subjects. But despite the availability of many high quality resources, the ability to physically attend classes remains an obstacle for many commercial mariners.

As a result, more and more schools are embracing online programs that enable students to take classes from any location with internet access. These are called distance learning, or virtual classroom programs. As with any form of education, people should find out if a program is approved by an official organization or government entity for accreditation purposes.

# *Commercial Mariners and Maritime Law*

When the *Titanic* sank in on its maiden voyage, the world was shocked by the tragic loss. In 1985, an American-French expedition team discovered the wreck site and created renewed public interest in the ill-fated liner. We learned that *Titanic* actually broke in two during its final moments, and that brittle steel may have played a role in the sinking. However, issues far more fundamental than the metallurgical quality of *Titanic's* rivets sealed the fate of over 1,500 people on the night of April 14, 1912.

These things included the lack of urgency given to ice warnings, the inadequate number of lifeboats, and possibly the decision to call for full astern in a desperate effort to avoid hitting the iceberg. Historians have since raised additional issues regarding confusion as to helm commands and the unavailability of binoculars for lookouts. While the countless "what-ifs" of that fateful night could be pondered forever, Walter Lord, author of *A Night to Remember*, probably summed it up best. He wrote, "It is a rash man indeed who would set himself up as final arbiter on all that happened the incredible night the *Titanic* went down." [61]

Despite the public's fascination with the sinking, most people aren't aware that it involved an unusual element of maritime law. As with any maritime disaster, lawsuits were filed. In response, *Titanic's* owners took steps to limit their losses. They did this by invoking an arcane concept of maritime law known as limitation of liability. Supreme Court Justice Oliver Wendell Holmes ruled in favor of the vessel interests, and allowed them to limit their liability (payments to victims) to the post-accident value of the liner. [62] Since the *Titanic* was sitting on the ocean floor in a spot that was two miles deep, the only thing left of its post-accident value was a flotilla of lifeboats worth about $92,000.

Limitation of liability is just one of the odd quirks of maritime law, which is the special body of law that governs activities on navigable waters. This covers the operation of ships, collision of ships, injuries to mariners, jurisdiction over ships, arrest of ships, damage to cargo, salvage, pollution, and related matters. This chapter highlights laws that are applicable to commercial mariners and maritime industry workers.

**The Jones Act** One of the most well-known maritime laws in the United States is the Jones Act. The Jones Act requires that commerce between U.S. ports be carried out by vessels that are:
- built in the United States
- owned by United States citizens
- operated under the U.S. flag
- manned by United States citizens or permanent residents

The architects of the Jones Act recognized that a strong merchant marine was important for the economy and for national security. The Jones Act was meant to provide U.S. shipyards with construction contracts and U.S. merchant mariners with jobs. In addition to vessel construction and operation, the Jones Act governs legal remedies for crewmembers injured on the job.

This part of the Jones Act is familiar to many commercial mariners. It covers seamen, which include commercial fishermen, tugboat deckhands, tanker captains, and others who are part of the crew of a U.S. flag vessel. To be a seaman, someone must (1.) contribute to the function of a vessel or to the accomplishment of its mission, and (2.) have a connection to a vessel in navigation (or to an identifiable group of vessels) that is substantial in terms of both its duration and its nature. [63] Through the Jones Act, an injured seaman could be entitled to compensation. This includes something called maintenance and cure. Maintenance covers living expenses and cure covers medical expenses.

**The Seaman's Protection Act** (46 U.S.C. 2114) was enacted to protect seamen and other people affected by maritime activity. The law forbids an employer from firing a seaman for refusing to perform duties if the seaman has a reasonable apprehension or expectation that carrying out such duties would result in serious injury to the seaman, other seamen, or the public. The Seaman's Protection Act was raised in a federal court case involving tows that were six barges long. Arguments were made that such long tows created safety problems.

**The Seaman's Manslaughter Statute** (18 U.S.C. 1115) was enacted in the 1800s to hold ship's personnel accountable for accidents that resulted in the death of passengers, crewmembers, or people on shore. The statute imposes up to ten years imprisonment, and possibly fines, if a wrongful act causes a loss of life. The Seaman's Manslaughter Statute was raised by authorities after a tragic fire aboard the steamer *General Slocum* claimed the lives of more than a thousand passengers in 1904.

**Longshore and Harbor Workers' Compensation Act (LHWCA)** The LHWCA provides compensation to employees injured in the course of traditional maritime employment on navigable waters who are NOT seamen. It operates similar to workers' compensation law. It covers mechanics, electricians, riggers, welders, stevedores, harbor pilots, and non-seaman divers.

 **Alcohol testing regulations introduce a difficult issue for crews.** Many vessels now carry alcohol testing kits. This is due to regulations that make it mandatory to conduct alcohol testing within two hours for anyone involved in a serious marine incident. On a small vessel, this could create a difficult situation where crewmembers are forced to test each other. Critics argue that this essentially amounts to self-policing.

Navigable waters include piers, bulkheads, drydocks, and similar structures. Traditional maritime employment includes ship repair, shipbuilding, shipbreaking, bunkering, cargo operations, marine construction, and commercial diving. If the injured person is a regular crewmember of a vessel, there is no coverage under the LHWCA, because the person would be considered a Jones Act seaman.

Coverage under the LHWCA would be denied if the sole cause of injury was the employee's intoxication, or employee's deliberate attempt to injure himself or another person. With some types of employees, it can sometimes be tricky to figure out whether the Jones Act or the LHWCA should apply. For instance, commercial divers often work on oil rigs in the Gulf of Mexico. They may become a regular part of a vessel's crew. Determining which law applies would depend on a diver's relationship to a vessel and time spent working on the vessel.

The **Outer Continental Shelf Lands Act** (OCSLA) covers people whose work involves exploration, development, removal, and transport of natural resources from the outer continental shelf region, which includes the seabed and areas beneath the seabed. OCSLA benefits include payment in the event of disability or death.

**Limitation of Liability** The Limitation of Shipowners' Liability Act of 1851 states that a shipowner may limit liability for losses from negligence or unseaworthiness arising without his privity and knowledge. "Privity" means participation and involvement. As mentioned earlier in the chapter, the law was invoked by the owners of the *Titanic*.

Limitation law was also used by the owners of the *Morro Castle* when it caught fire and foundered off Asbury Park, New Jersey on September 9, 1935. The fire claimed the lives of 137 passengers and crew. When the liner's owners succeeded in limiting their liability to the charred remains of the ship, worth about $20,000 at the time, it stirred negative public sentiments.

This led to the creation of a limitation fund of $60 per ton salvaged, which was raised to $420 per ton in 1984. The law has many critics who claim it is used in instances that were never envisioned by its creators. Back in the nineteenth century, shipowners needed an incentive to operate the clipper ships that fostered commerce. Without limitation law, a shipowner could be wiped out by cargo losses that exceeded the value of a ship.

However, the law has been raised in cruise ship accidents, personal watercraft accidents, and other instances where there is arguably no connection to mercantile growth. Critics point out that electronic navigation, reliable diesel engines, and other developments have given shipowners greater control over the operation of their vessels, thereby eliminating the justification for protection offered by the law. Limitation of liability can be a contentious legal issue among maritime attorneys.

**Under limitation law, a shipowner could limit claimants' awards** to the post-casualty value of a vessel. On October 15, 2003, the ferry *Andrew Barberi* crashed into St. George Terminal. It was traveling at about 16 knots, roughly its normal sea speed. As this photo shows, the impact was devastating. It resulted in 11 deaths and more than 60 injuries. In the lawsuits that followed, the City of New York unsuccessfully attempted to limit claimants' awards to $14.4 million, which represented the value of the ferry after the accident.

**Maritime Law Presumptions** Maritime law presents commercial mariners with a number of interesting presumptions. A presumption is a legal premise that we accept at face value. For instance, criminal justice systems are supposed to operate by the presumption that a defendant is innocent unless proven guilty.

A commonly raised maritime law presumption is the *Pennsylvania Rule*. According to the rule, if a vessel involved in an accident violated a safety standard governed by statute, the operator has the burden of demonstrating that violation of the statute could not have caused the accident. If two vessels collide at night, and one of them was not displaying running lights, the vessel without running lights would have the burden of demonstrating that its failure to display running lights did not contribute to the accident.

Another commonly applied presumption is the **Oregon Rule**. It states that when a moving vessel hits a stationary object or vessel, there is a presumption that the moving vessel is at fault. But there's a twist to the Oregon Rule. The operator of the moving vessel can shift blame to the stationary vessel by arguing that it presented a hazard to navigation. This is often the case where barges and construction support vessels are left alongside bridges during extended maintenance or repairs. If such stationary vessels were not adequately illuminated at night, or if they were tied in a manner that obstructed passage under the bridge, it makes a strong case in favor of the moving vessel.

**Negligence** is the underlying basis of lawsuits involving collisions, crewmember injuries, passenger injuries, or cargo damages. A lawsuit based on negligence hinges on four elements. The first is the existence of a legal duty. The second is a breach of that duty. The third is that someone is injured, or that something is damaged. The fourth is that breach of the legal duty causes the injuries or damages.

Here's an illustration. A captain has a legal duty to operate a passenger ferry in a safe manner. He fails to reduce speed after fog sets in. This amounts to a breach of duty. As a result, he collides with an outbound cruise ship. Failure to reduce speed in fog was the breach of duty that caused the collision.

**Comparative Negligence** This element of maritime law governs how liability is shared among vessels or parties in an accident or other legal matter. The term *liability* essentially means *blame* or *fault*. In a collision between multiple vessels, liability is apportioned according to how much each vessel contributed to the collision.

A court will consider violations of collision regulations, safety regulations, errors in seamanship, influence of alcohol or drugs, equipment failure, communication problems, and actions taken by each vessel to avoid collision. Collisions on navigable waters tend to be more complex than those on land, with a greater possibility of blame being shared among multiple parties.

**Criminal Prosecutions** are legal proceedings that take place when the conduct of a commercial mariner results in a violation deemed to be *criminal*, as opposed to *civil*, in nature. In such proceedings, a federal or state prosecutor makes arguments before a court as to why a defendant should be punished. Criminal prosecutions in the maritime industry have increased because of a trend known as *criminalization*. This means that violations that were once considered civil in nature are now treated as crimes.

A good illustration of the concept of criminalization is the act of driving while intoxicated. Decades ago, people drank all night long at parties and then got into their cars to drive home. Sometimes the trip home was uneventful, and sometimes it ended in a tragic accident. Because of awareness campaigns throughout the country, drunk driving went from being considered just a social folly to being treated as a crime.

The distinction between treating something as a civil violation and a crime is a profound one. A civil violation could be something along the lines of failing to fill out administrative paperwork. The result might be that the offender is fined by a government agency. In contrast, a crime is a *felony* or *misdemeanor*, which means the possibility of imprisonment, not to mention greater chances for revocation or suspension of a license.

But what kind of conduct on the part of a commercial mariner rises to the level of a crime? A crime consists of two elements. The first element is that a person commits a criminal act. The second element is that the person acts with a requisite mental state. A criminal act is conduct that is prohibited in society. Murdering someone, threatening someone, breaking into a store at night… these are obvious criminal acts.

The element of mental state hinges on whether a person had the necessary state of mind to be considered a criminal. In general, there are four levels of mental states. These consist of acting: (i.) intentionally, (ii.) knowingly, (iii.) recklessly, or (iv.) with criminal negligence. When a person acts *intentionally*, he acts voluntarily and deliberately. If he sets fire to a rival company's tour boat in the middle of the night, he exhibits an *intentional* state of mind to commit the crime of arson.

If a criminal acts *knowingly*, he is reasonably certain of the consequences of his actions. Let's say a dredging supervisor uses dynamite charges to destroy a sunken barge. If he knows that salvage divers are working fifty yards away, and that divers could suffer ear injuries from the underwater blasting, he is acting *knowingly*.

It wouldn't matter that he turned to his deckhand and said, "I hope these dynamite charges don't injure those divers, because it's definitely not my intention to hurt anyone here. I'm just trying to destroy a sunken barge." That ridiculous statement would do nothing to lessen the guilt of the demolition contractor. Acting knowingly is sometimes described as *willful blindness*.

This scenario should further illustrate the concept. Let's say a mate is aware that a deckhand is menacing and threatening another deckhand in a psychological bullying situation.

**Can issues involving engine maintenance lead to criminal prosecution?**
Yes. In December 2004, the bulk carrier *Selendang Ayu* ran aground while en route from Seattle, Washington to Xiamen, China. The ship encountered Force 11 seas shortly after passing through the Strait of Juan De Fuca, and later suffered a cracked cylinder head in its main engine. After losing power, it ran aground off Unalaska Island, in the Aleutian Islands. The grounding caused the release of 340,000 gallons of fuel oil, resulting in damage to wildlife and prosecutions by the U.S. Attorney under the Refuse Act and the Migratory Bird Treaty Act. The U.S. Attorney argued that the engine was improperly maintained, after concluding that the crack was caused by thermal loading from failing to seal and clean cylinders, aggravated by fuel injection timing and turbocharger issues. 64

The mate pretends not be aware of the problem because she doesn't want to get dragged into an unpleasant confrontation. She figures that the bully deckhand will eventually be transferred off her boat. Her inaction would be considered willful blindness.

The third state of mind is *recklessness*. This means that someone recognizes a risk in his irresponsible conduct, yet chooses to ignore it. Let's say the operator of a small utility skiff gets a big kick out of buzzing a towboat saddled down with sixteen barges. The furious towboat captain jumps out of the wheelhouse swinging his fists and screaming obscenities. But that only amuses the troublemaker and encourages him further. The operator of the skiff is acting recklessly because he recognizes the danger created by his conduct, yet continues his actions.

The fourth state of mind is acting with *criminal negligence*. The test for criminal negligence resembles the test for *recklessness*. However, with criminal negligence, the wrongdoer doesn't recognize the risk in his conduct. Think of a newly formed marine transportation company that purchases a fleet of old workboats at dirt cheap prices. Excited about their bargain, the owners have the interiors of the boats stripped to make room for new diesels and auxiliary systems.

All the gutted mechanical and electrical systems are thrown into dumpsters and sent to the local landfill. Government authorities arrest the new owners for violations of numerous environmental statutes, including those for asbestos disposal, PCB disposal, and air emissions. The new owners are dumbfounded to learn that their newly acquired vessels contained asbestos insulation and PCB-filled electrical equipment in the machinery spaces. Their conduct can be considered *criminal negligence* because they didn't recognize the hazard.

Sometimes it's what someone *doesn't do* that can lead to trouble. The prosecution of unlawful oil discharges by the U.S. Department of Justice clearly fits into the realm of intentional crimes. The act of inserting a "magic pipe" to bypass an oily water separator is a voluntary and deliberate act. However, crews have also been prosecuted for *failure to maintain entries* in the oily waste logbook, an official document intended to provide a record of a vessel's waste management practices.

**Environmental Violations** There is a vast body of environmental law that applies to commercial mariners, codified in regulations of the U.S. Coast Guard, U.S. Environmental Protection Agency, and other federal, state, and municipal agencies. These laws impose penalties for spills involving petroleum and other hazardous substances. Some of the better known laws include MARPOL regulations, the Oil Pollution Act of 1990 (also known as OPA 90), Clean Water Act, Refuse Act, and Migratory Bird Treaty Act.

Many of today's environmental laws carry criminal penalties for violations. And with some laws, commercial mariners could be prosecuted even if they didn't act with a criminal state of mind. This could be the case where laws impose strict liability. In other words, it doesn't matter that a commercial mariner did or didn't act recklessly or negligently. The fact that a spill took place is all that might be required to result in prosecution.

**Marine Salvage Laws** In maritime law, a salvage claim can arise if these three elements are met: (1.) A vessel is in peril, (2.) There is a voluntary act on the part of a rescuer (salvor) to assist the vessel, and (3.) The rescue venture is successful. A salvage claim is generally a percentage of the value of the rescued vessel. Any vessel, from a yacht club tender to a tanker, can act as a salvor.

Salvage law is rooted in the concept that mariners who come to the aid of a stricken vessel should have some incentive for doing so. The salvor might change course, lose time in his own voyage, and experience spoilage of cargo. The concept dates back to ancient times. Salvage rights do not materialize if there was a pre-existing duty to respond, as in the case of a vessel contracted to provide towing services.

**Although modern technology has enabled commercial mariners** to control many of the traditional perils of going to sea, salvage claims can still materialize in modern times. You could offer assistance to a stricken vessel, and surprisingly find yourself entitled to a salvage award. On the flip side, if your vessel breaks down, you might have to follow the home office's instructions in entering agreements with a responding vessel. That can mean negotiating whether a rescue effort will be treated as services billed at an hourly rate, or whether it will be considered a salvage matter, where the salvor can assert a claim for a percentage of the rescued vessel's value.

Despite it's ancient roots, salvage law has been shaped by modern events. If a salvor's efforts avert environmental damage to surrounding shores, that could be considered as an element in calculating a salvage award. This development came about with the Salvage Convention of 1989, which materialized about eleven years after the *Amoco Cadiz* oil spill.

In March 1978, the 230,000 ton *Amoco Cadiz* caused a major oil spill off the Brittany Coast after foundering on a reef during ferocious sea conditions. The tanker experienced a failure of its steering gear. The salvage tug *Pacific* made great efforts to attach a towing chain to the stricken tanker and ultimately succeeded. However, the severe weather conditions were too much for the towing gear, which parted during efforts to pull the tanker into deeper water. [65]

# *Creating Job Security for Yourself*

There was once a time when society was carefree and people casually changed jobs without so much as a second thought. Life was good, and it was commonplace to leave one employer for another in pursuit of better salaries, benefits, or working conditions. The world hadn't yet become as lean and mean as it is today, and there were plenty of lucrative pickings to go around for everyone.

Society was still enjoying the momentum of a powerful post-war economy that provided prosperity into the 1960s and 1970s. Well, things have changed. Companies have downsized. Populations have swelled. And for the most part, life has become more competitive in the maritime industry, as it has in most places.

While there are plenty of good jobs available, there's a virtually endless pool of applicants waiting in line to fill them. The heartless reality of supply and demand has pounded down salaries everywhere. And that's why it's important to hold on to a good job with a good company. This isn't meant to come off in a "lecturing" sort of tone.

It's only meant as sound advice, because some companies are really good deals, while others are not. And that's something one learns through experience. There are a number of ways to preserve a good job. One of the best ways is to be positive and to work hard. 'Sorry for sounding like Mother Goose, because we know life isn't that simple.

**If a newcomer doesn't catch on quickly to the concept** of securing watertight doors and hatches, veteran crewmembers will get the message across, in no uncertain terms and without too much finesse or subtleness. Failure to secure watertight doors and hatches in heavy seas can be fatal. In the early morning hours of April 2, 2001, the fishing vessel *Arctic Rose* sank in the Bering Sea with the tragic loss of fifteen lives. The U.S. Coast Guard investigation revealed an open weathertight door toward the vessel's stern. It was theorized that large amounts of water poured into fish processing spaces through the open door as the vessel ran downwind in following seas. 66 Commercial vessels are generally constructed of steel. If watertight integrity is compromised by open doors and hatches, the entry of seawater will quickly put an end to a vessel's buoyancy.

The real world offers us work settings with their fair share of personal alliances, cliques, feuds, and other forms of politics that one must deal with to get through the day. It would be unrealistic and insincere to suggest that a few pages of trite advice could prepare one for such challenges. Perhaps experience and confidence are the best defenses here, and those come with time. But until one acquires those attributes, the smartest approach is to work hard and not let things get the better of you.

After all, there's no shortage of adversities on a commercial vessel. Working conditions can be dangerous. Watchstanding schedules can be physically and mentally depleting. It can be difficult to catch sleep at times. Extremes of weather can take their toll on the body. And of course, some co-workers can be difficult.

Working hard won't make such adversities disappear. But it can earn a person respect among shipmates. It can make co-workers more inclined to accept you and teach you things. And it can strengthen job security by creating favorable impressions. In the beginning, that can mean giving more than 100% when you come aboard a vessel. This isn't to imply that it's okay to slack off once you've become comfortable. It's just a reminder that newcomers are closely watched. And newcomers tend to be judged more quickly or harshly than everyone else.

Don't let the antics of others get you down. Let's say you're a new deckhand assigned to painting a barge deck. Everything's going fine as you're working alongside a couple of other deckhands. Suddenly, at the sound of the mate's footsteps, one of the deckhands comes alive and says, "C'mon guys, we've been on this spot all morning. Let's stop the chit chat and pick up the pace!"

A casual observer might think, "Wow, what leadership qualities that guy has. He's really serious about getting the job done." On the other hand, many co-workers would more likely think, "What a clown! He's trying to make himself look good at our expense. This is someone to be careful around."

But people like that can be found in every workplace. You can't be demoralized by such things. Superiors generally recognize such people for what they are. A job is a daily trial of interaction with all sorts of people. Some are going to be nice, while others are not. This is true whether you work at a hardware store, catering house, or pet shop.

And don't let unfriendly people defeat your confidence in others on a vessel. There will be many people who are decent. If you work hard and wait until the time is right to learn things, many shipmates will be helpful. Some might be reluctant to share their knowledge because it could undermine their authority or exclusivity with certain tasks. But those types of people are everywhere. You'll find plenty of co-workers who are nice, helpful, and who enjoy teaching newcomers.

On a commercial vessel, being punctual is critical. If someone arrives 30 minutes late at an office job with an insurance company, it's not the end of the world. Although it doesn't look good, that person could make up for it by working into her lunch break or staying a little late at the end of the day to give the company a square deal for a day's pay. But being late on a boat can mean half a dozen people costing the company forty bucks an hour are ticking away on the clock.

Meanwhile, a boat that's worth $2,000 a day isn't making a cent for the company because it's waiting for a straggler. That doesn't go over well. Neither does being unprepared. Showing up on time, but not having the necessary gear to stand a watch in the engine room won't score points with superiors. It doesn't look good to run into the galley and rummage through cabinets and drawers while frantically asking the cook if he knows where to find an extra pair of work gloves.

This industry sometimes gets admonished for drug or substance abuse. That isn't fair. People who work on commercial vessels are generally hardworking folks who just want to get through the day without trouble so they can support their families.

**Of all the staggering technical data for a cruise ship like *Liberty of the Seas,*** perhaps the most relevant statistic for jobseekers is that there are about 1,360 crew positions onboard. At 154,407 tons, *Liberty of the Seas* is a good example of a very large cruise ship. The 18 deck vessel is 1,112 feet long, 184 feet wide, and draws 28 feet of water. Six 17,000 horsepower Wärtsilä 46V12 diesels drive electric generators, which provide power to three pods, two of which are azimuthing. Fuel consumption is about 28,000 gallons per hour. There are 1,817 staterooms for 4,375 passengers. The $947 million ship offers many amenities intended to delight passengers, such as a waterpark with three pools, surf simulator, ice skating rink, rock climbing wall, miniature golf course, and jogging course. 67

Commercial mariners know that drugs or alcohol would kill a career in a heartbeat. Drug possession can also lead to criminal prosecution. With all the hard work it takes to land a good job, no one wants to throw all that away.

On commercial vessels, companies have zero-tolerance policies about alcohol. There may be boats where drinking with the crew on shore is okay, as in the case of a yacht in an exciting resort. But even there, moderation is important.

Going ashore together in foreign ports, crews can grow close. But if a yacht owner sees a new steward throwing up a night's worth of beers before coming back on board, it doesn't bode well for job security.

**How can I get one of those high paying jobs on a fishing boat?** In recent years, many people have become interested in commercial fishing jobs, probably in no small part due to popular television shows such as *Deadliest Catch, Lobster Wars, or Big Shrimpin.'* Over beers at the local bar, friends may hear stories of deckhands making a year's wages in a few months during the crab season in the Aleutian Islands. The natural response might be, "I want a piece of that!" However, it isn't that easy to get a job on a crab boat out of Dutch Harbor. It's a close-knit labor pool where there aren't frequent vacancies, and the ones that do arise are often filled by family or friends. People who want to break into the industry often explore positions on fish processing facilities. These vacancies are more common and sometimes provide opportunities to meet captains and mates from fishing vessels. In the photo above, the Gulf shrimper with a wooden pilothouse and delicate looking outriggers might suggest a gentler way of life than the brutal and cold Bering Sea. But don't be fooled. Shrimping in the Gulf is tough work, in terms of long hours, oppressive heat, violent squalls, and the tedious drudgery of mending fishing nets.

It's important for people to realize they aren't on a training ship. It's easy for a new employee to be burning with desire to learn as much as possible to obtain a license and advance quickly. But employees should never lose sight of the fact that their primary responsibility is to work. There will be plenty of time to learn. If someone acts apathetically toward tasks that don't deliver educational benefits, it could foster resentment from superiors.

Most captains, mates, and senior engineers invested lots of time to get where they are. They spent years on the water. They sacrificed plenty of weekends studying for licenses. They could have spent thousands of dollars on training courses and books. Such veterans of the industry won't have much patience for someone who acts as if every assignment should be a classroom learning experience.

It's said that no one is indispensable. As condescending as that might sound, it's true. Someone might be a real hotshot when it comes to pulling rabbits out of hats. He might be the one who always knows what to do, whether it's pulling off a tricky fuel transfer to eliminate a starboard list, or setting radar alarms that no one else can seem to figure out. But anyone can be replaced.

And true to the tired expression, honesty is always a good policy. It's better to be straightforward than to try bluffing through tough situations. If you're on watch in the engine room and the chief comes down and asks why you didn't swap lube oil coolers like he instructed in the night order book, tell the truth. If you forgot to do so, admit it. Such oversight might not impress the chief.

But it's worse to fabricate something like, "Well, chief, I tried to swap them, but the seawater outlet valve on the upper cooler was jammed." If the chief realizes that wasn't the case, you'll lose his trust, which could take a long time to restore. It's better to say, "Chief, I'm sorry. I must have missed that entry. I'll swap coolers as soon as the wiper returns from sounding tanks."

The unique conditions aboard a vessel can provide opportunities to see the best and worst of co-workers, more so than in many shoreside settings. With jobs on shore, people only have to work together for eight hours a day. At five o'clock, they say good night and go home to their families. But on a vessel, co-workers often work AND live together, which can be more demanding on interpersonal skills.

That means working on commercial vessels requires thoughtfulness. So does life in general. But a lack of thoughtfulness will show itself more conspicuously on a commercial vessel. Utmost courtesy is required towards shipmates and roommates. This can mean walking on eggshells if you enter a cabin while a roommate is sleeping.

You could work staggered schedules where one of you sleeps while the other stands watch. Try not to drop things like keys, coins, or belt buckles. Such things falling on vinyl floor tiles can wake people up. If living like this seems like too much to ask for, think about nuclear submarines, where people might have to hot bunk. A submarine could go to sea with more crewmembers than places to sleep. Someone coming off watch could have to crawl into the bunk his relief just got out of, hence the expression. Not even having your own bunk... that could make any hardship seem easy in comparison!

It's important to keep bathrooms, or heads as they're called on vessels, clean. On small vessels, cleaning toilets is often the responsibility of junior deckhands. But junior or senior, no one enjoys stooping down to retrieve crumpled up paper towels from under a toilet bowl. Keeping such areas clean is part of being a considerate shipmate. The same goes for the galley. If someone takes the last cup of coffee from the pot left out by the cook, it would be thoughtful to make a fresh pot for the next person.

When getting food in the galley, the rule on many boats is similar to armed forces doctrine. That is, "Take what you want, but eat what you take." With people starving throughout the world, it's not as if there ARE places where it's okay to be wasteful with food. However, waste on a vessel can have a more profound impact in terms of depleting stores. A cook can't jump on the tender and run ashore to the nearest supermarket for pancake mix or mayonnaise.

Be positive, and express an interest in learning new things. While it was mentioned earlier that a commercial vessel isn't a training ship, this could be tempered with the notion that learning is an ever-present thing. One doesn't need to be in a lecture hall to learn. Learning can be a spur-of-the-moment tutorial from a bosun about how to make an eye splice. It could be a two-minute lesson from a mate about how to download updates for an electronic chart. Always be receptive to learning. That will make you valuable and help solidify your security.

Don't violate the chain of command. If you signed on as a tankerman and are displeased with the fact that your requests for protective gear are scoffed at, don't start making phone calls to the operations superintendent's office. Follow established protocol.

If you're supposed to speak with the mate or captain, follow that route. Safety should come first as a guiding principle on all boats, and you should never be pressured to compromise your safety, or the safety of others. But if there's a problem, it's important to remember the chain of command.

And if you're unhappy about something on a boat, don't go complaining to everyone around you. You may be new and other crew members could be seen as having paid their dues. Entry-level crew members aren't always entering a democracy, or at least a democracy where they're considered voting members. It's easy to complain about a million different things, whether you're a captain or a deckhand...

"We're working New Years Eve again this year? That's not fair. We worked it last year!"

"This company is so cheap! Tell me they can't spend a couple of bucks for some non-skid panels on the foredeck!"

"Some job. I'm learning so much... like how to chip paint and rust!"

Voicing complaints in an unwise manner could backfire. To begin with, you might not be complaining to sympathetic ears. The person listening to you might not care that you're not learning things you thought you'd be learning. They might nod as they think to themselves, "Well, no one told you this was a training seminar for you to learn electronic navigation. You came here to work, buddy."

Another thing is that useless complaining can make its way to the wrong ears, and that can undermine job security. If things warrant criticism, there are constructive ways to voice concern or dissatisfaction. For instance, saying something like, "I'm concerned about this practice of sending someone into an empty tank without a safety person around."

"If she passes out from fumes, no one will know and she could die down there. I think we should think about assigning a safety person to accompany her." That's a whole lot better than saying, "This standard operating procedure for tank inspection stinks. Someone's gonna get killed because this company is too cheap to value our safety!"

Some of these things are common sense. Some come with experience. Whatever the case may be, if you're ever not sure of how to handle a tough situation, it could be a good policy to stop and think for a moment how your words and actions could affect your job.

# *Am I Cut Out for This Line of Work?*

What are the chances you'll enjoy working on a commercial vessel? Different folks walk away with different impressions of their experiences on the water. Many have stepped aboard their first boat without ever looking back. The job provided a means to buy a first home, start a family, and build a wonderful life.

There are thirty-five-year-olds who are saying, "Look at me… I started out as deckhand ten years ago after realizing that college wasn't for me. I walked into my first interview armed with nothing but a high school diploma. But I worked hard. I studied hard, both in the company's in-house training programs, and on my own with license prep courses."

"I eventually got my 1600 ton license and now I make $85,000 a year as captain of a towboat pushing barges on the Mississippi River. I work four weeks on and two weeks off. I have eggs over easy and hash browns in the morning, compliments of our devoted cook. I've got two beautiful kids, a brand new minivan, and my husband and I are looking into a bigger house. Most people who've finished grad school haven't attained the quality of life I've been able to provide for my family. It doesn't get any better than this. Someone pinch me so I know this isn't a dream!"

And then there are forty-year-olds out there saying, "I can't believe I signed up for this. My fingers are numb from reeling in smelly fishing nets all day long. I'm sharing a cabin with someone who snores all night long. I'm a hundred miles off New Bedford and my back is killing me. I should have bought the larger size container of Motrin at the drug store. I'm running on cereal and powdered milk for breakfast and microwave pizza for dinner. I know there are people in the world who go to bed hungry, but I thought shipboard meals were a big part of maintaining crew morale. I guess that doesn't apply on this boat."

"It's hard to sleep because my bunk is two feet aft of the forepeak chain locker and this boat pitches like a bronco all night long. The only reason I fall asleep on my thin damp mattress is because I'm too exhausted to keep my eyes open at the end of the day. What a tale of adventure to tell my grandchildren. Ah, the thrill of going to sea!"

Working on a commercial vessel can result in different sentiments for different folks. Youth is a big factor in shaping one's outlook about the industry. People who are young and open-minded are more likely to roll with the punches and deal with the adversities of working on the water. If someone is middle-aged and no longer flexible enough deal with relentless work schedules and an absence of privacy, going to sea could be a bitter experience. If you take a twenty-year-old and a forty-year-old and put them into the same position of cruise ship waiter, you're likely to get differing impressions from each.

The younger waiter is more likely to acclimate to the difficult routine of sharing a small cabin in the bowels of a cruise ship with a couple of strangers. The young crewmember might take a lot of things in stride and shake off aggravation by touring a foreign port with shipmates. The older crewmember would be more likely to get agitated when a roommate turned on the ceiling light to search for socks at 1:00 a.m. instead of using a flashlight.

**This photo of a diesel generator might not convey what it's like** to work in the engine room of a tug, ferry, megayacht, or fishing vessel. However, it's important to appreciate a few realities about these places. Diesel engines are loud. They produce lots of vibration. The air around them can be thick with fuel and oil vapors. It can easily reach 110°F when things are humming. Studying license questions about diesel injectors and centrifugal governors is one thing, while standing watches in hot and loud machinery spaces like this is something else. Designated duty engineer, qualified member of the engineering department, third assistant engineer... those are merely titles. Places like this are where those people punch their time cards.

The older crewmember wouldn't find much camaraderie in competing with three roommates for a turn at a small sink, especially if he's rushing to get to a breakfast serving station... and the dining room supervisor already scolded him for being late the day before.

To be happy working on a boat, it helps if people know something about the routine they're getting into. For one thing, commercial boats are run by an organizational structure that's not unlike those aboard naval vessels. Commands are given and commands are expected to be followed.

**What's the difference between a tugboat and a towboat?** They both accomplish the same mission, which is pushing or pulling barges. Tugboats are usually oval or elliptical in shape when viewed from above, while towboats tend to be rectangular. Viewed from the side, tugs generally exhibit a noticeable curve, or sheer, culminating in a high bow. In contrast, towboats tend to have a relatively flat profile. Tugboats operate in inland waters, coastal waters, and offshore. In contrast, towboats operate in rivers and inland waters. Towboats are usually low in the water, since designers don't worry about tons of solid green water being dumped on their decks. Towboats tend to have "knees," which are those triangular structures at the bow that take the brunt of forces in pushing barges. However, you see them on tugs sometimes. Both types of vessels can be single or twin-screwed. While you won't often see a triple-screw tug, three engines aren't an uncommon configuration on large towboats.

Although the drill doesn't involve salutes and regulation haircuts, it involves a strict code of conduct. Commands can be given brusquely, or they can be given softly and politely. That's a personal quality of a captain or mate. Nevertheless, a commercial vessel isn't a place where communication is necessarily carried out with delicate manners.

Small vessels tend to be loud places when their engines are running. High winds and swells can make for a hazardous work platform. Jockeying a 100' steel tug alongside a barge in adverse conditions requires concentration. And such situations don't lend themselves to a gentle school of communications etiquette. Someone might be told, "Coil up that line on the foredeck," or "Tell that new deckhand to get off the stern, now!" Such directness isn't necessarily out of rudeness.

Things need to be conveyed clearly and quickly. A soft-spoken mate might instead say, "Why don't we coil up that line," or "Let's get that new deckhand off the stern. He could get hurt." But one's feelings shouldn't be ruffled if the words "please" or "could you" are left out when given an order or request. The higher priority is on giving commands that don't leave room for misunderstanding or ambiguity.

That doesn't mean a supervisory position is a license to abuse subordinates. Everyone deserves to be treated with dignity, even if they just stepped aboard a boat and don't know port from starboard. Companies shouldn't tolerate abusive officers who are unnecessarily heavy-handed with their authority. Nor should companies tolerate officers who intimidate subordinates into carrying out orders of questionable wisdom.

If someone is asked to drill holes in a bulkhead with a high-speed drill, she should be given eye protection to guard against steel splinters or a shattering drill bit. If someone is asked to use a rotary stripper to grind away rust, he should be given respiratory protection to prevent breathing in clouds of iron oxide dust. Workers shouldn't be scoffed at for requesting safety equipment. Everyone deserves to be worked fairly and safely.

But just like in any workplace, whether it's a construction site or a supermarket, there are all kinds of leaders. There are kind supervisors and there are mean ones. There are officers who are the mentoring type.

**I gotta have my olive bread and organic eggs for breakfast.** When it comes to chow time, some people are more particular than others. Wholesome food can mean different things to different people. For some, a heaping plate of canned ravioli or fried chicken can be major comfort food. For others, such food is unthinkable, because they're accustomed to hormone-free chicken, exotic salads, and specialty breads. Well, many commercial boats are simply not stocked with food of the latter type. Therefore, going to sea can mean relinquishing some control over what you eat. Since reputable ship operators provide food which is nutritious and appetizing, this isn't really a big issue for most people. While it costs more to provide quality food instead of high-starch fare, there are dividends for vessel operators in terms of crew performance, alertness, and morale. This is an area which has seen greater attention with Crew Endurance Management (CEM) programs.

And there are officers who feel that they learned things the hard way. Therefore, everyone should go through the ordeals they went through. The type of supervisor you wind up with is often a matter of luck. And that can be a big factor in loving a job or hating it.

Another important point is that no one should be expected to violate the law. In this business, that's easier to do than it sounds. Violating the law doesn't necessarily mean drinking vodka from a hidden bottle in your cabin, or lighting up a marijuana joint on the stern at night.

Those types of things would end a career anywhere... on a commercial boat, in a corporate office, or in a factory. But on a commercial boat, it's easy to unknowingly break the law by failing to follow safety protocols or failing to comply with environmental regulations.

Quality of life issues can strongly impact whether a person likes or dislikes working on a boat. This area has been the focus of greater attention than in the past, largely due to CEM, or Crew Endurance Management programs. The broad issue of crew endurance is impacted, directly or indirectly, by a host of factors. These include cabin quality, food quality, potable water quality, exercise equipment, and recreational outlets.

The well-being and comfort of employees is more than just a casual consideration for employers. Companies realize that crews who live in good environments are less prone to make mistakes, whether it's a pilot docking a towboat or a deckhand keeping a lookout in crowded shipping lanes. This makes for fewer injuries, fewer groundings, fewer collisions, and fewer environmental incidents.

Reputable companies invest in creature comforts for their employees. This includes nutritious and well-balanced meals, good quality potable water, clean bed sheets, and decently insulated cabins to shut out noise from engines and crew traffic in passageways.

However, these things are not a universal attribute of all boats. There are vessels where potable water tanks, living quarters, and other habitability considerations are not conducive to maintaining well-rested and well-nourished crews. It can depend on the age of a vessel and the budget of a company.

**Do I need to have genuine concerns about piracy?** The vast majority of commercial mariners will go through their careers without ever experiencing a piracy incident. However, just as the vast majority of motorists will go through life without having a catastrophic car accident, it only takes one to ruin your day. The severity of piracy threats depends on the region. There are piracy hot spots, perhaps the most well-known of which lie in the waters surrounding Somalia. This region captured worldwide attention with the hijacking of the *Maersk Alabama* in 2009. However, piracy is a worldwide problem. Pirates operate in the Strait of Malacca, Indian Ocean, and Caribbean. The public knows less about these other regions because the incidents don't always appear in the evening news.

Companies realize that providing recreational outlets can keep people happy. And people who are happy tend to be more attentive on watch. They tend to make fewer mistakes and are less prone to depression or boredom. That's why some companies furnish exercise bikes, free weights, and treadmills. On large ships of an earlier era, crews sometimes enjoyed small swimming pools, especially on Middle East oil routes.

Recreational amenities can depend upon what a company feels is reasonable in terms of internet access, e-mail, satellite television, movie CDs, libraries, and video games. The significance of these things could be lost on someone who lives 10 minutes from work, swims a few laps at the gym after work, enjoys a cold beer at dinner with the family, and then watches TV after the kids go to bed.

But for a commercial mariner who's far from loved ones for weeks on end, every little thing can make a difference... from the cheerful atmosphere of a crew pizza night to doing a few 150 mph laps on a NASCAR video game. Happiness can also have a lot to do with the type of shipmates you get.

You could work with people who would open their homes to you if you were far from loved ones during the holidays, and you could work with people who still act like strangers after being shipmates for six months. But that's life. People are people wherever you go, and commercial vessels are like any other work setting.

Smoking can be a sticky point on some vessels. Although our society has become intolerant towards second-hand smoke, smoking protocols aboard commercial vessels can be a different matter. Some employers ban smoking on their vessels altogether. Some allow smoking in outdoor areas. On commercial vessels, the expectation of a "smoke-free" workplace is something that depends on company policy, how effectively company policy is enforced, and overall crew attitude towards second-hand smoke.

Oh, and let's not forget about that important issue of money. This line of work won't make anyone a millionaire. For those who are willing to work hard, study hard, and pass licenses exams, they can make good money with the right company. This can mean the ability to support a family and buy a house if they stay the course and advance their careers.

**Working on tankers can mean long periods at sea.** A stint on an inland vessel could run four weeks, two weeks, or a couple of days. On a large tanker, a stint could run two or three months, if not longer. The tanker industry is a good place to find superlatives in terms of vessel dimensions. The *Hellespont Alhambra*, now named the *T1 Asia*, is among a handful of the largest tankers in the world. Built in 2002, the 441,585 ton ship is 1,202 feet in length. [68] The modern supertanker is a product of the economies of scale. In naval architecture, the mathematical relationship between a ship's linear dimensions and internal volume is cubic in nature. In other words, the carrying capacity goes up as the cube of a vessel's length. However, crewing costs remain more or less constant, as it takes roughly the same number of deck and engine personnel to man a 400,000 ton tanker as it does a 60,000 ton tanker.

But for those who are in the game only for the money, there are better and safer pathways to wealth. Money shouldn't be the sole factor for entering this industry. However, we all know it often is for many folks. And that's not because people are misguided or naive. It's because the chance to earn a six-figure income as a senior deck or engine officer can be extremely enticing, especially when decent jobs on shore become scarcer by the day.

Getting back to the question at the beginning of the chapter about whether you'll enjoy working on a commercial vessel… it's a difficult question to answer. Unless a person has been on a commercial boat, he or she can only guess at the answer. There are people who love this line of work, and there are people who hate it. And because life is complex, it's not always such a black or white answer. These jobs have elements that are good and they have elements that are bad.

**Every type of commercial vessel** has its own unique hazards. On tugboats, a hawser that snaps can cut a person in two. On tankers, an empty cargo hold with low oxygen levels could lead to asphyxiation. The most dangerous sector of the industry is commercial fishing. In 2010, the Coast Guard found that more than 40 people die annually during commercial fishing operations. The commercial fishing industry accounted for 27% of commercial mariner deaths and injuries over a five-year period. [69]

So instead of simply loving or hating a job, it could be a matter of loving the overtime pay… but hating the grueling watch schedules. It could be a matter of loving navigation and seamanship… but hating to share a cabin with a grumpy shipmate. It could be about respecting the concept of working hard… but resenting the fact that some people get away without working hard while others don't.

Although nothing short of rolling up your sleeves and signing aboard a vessel can provide a taste of the industry, there are some things you could do beforehand to help answer this question. For starters, you must know yourself well and have realistic expectations. After all, even if you've never worked on a boat before, you know a thing or two about yourself. If someone likes his privacy and solitude, he should give some thought to whether he is suited to sharing a cabin with two or three strangers.

If someone suffers a week of debilitating back pain after shoveling snow for an hour, he should have second thoughts about the long and strenuous demands of life as a deckhand. If someone is fortunate enough to recognize her aversion to high levels of heat, noise, and vibration, she could wisely use that awareness to avoid a job in the engineering department. Never mind the fact that a second assistant engineer on a large container ship could earn $75,000 a year. People need to be comfortable in their work settings.

Readers can also comb the Internet to get an idea of how others feel about working on commercial vessels. People who've worked in the industry sometimes post their experiences in websites, chat rooms, and forums. These can be the cyber equivalents of water coolers, where crews from tugboats, cruise ships, and other vessels gather to swap stories. Some writers express their experiences with refrained literary style, while others do it with obscenity-laced sentiments.

If you know someone who works on a local vessel, you could ask to hitch a ride for a couple of hours. Someone could do lots of book and internet research to learn what it's like to work on commercial vessels, but seeing what it's like firsthand is different. Even if you don't know someone in the industry, you could invest a couple of dollars to take a ride on a local ferry or water taxi to observe crewmembers in action.

You could approach the captain or mate and ask to see the wheelhouse or engine room. They could decline your request because of company policy. But if things aren't stressfully busy, and you explain why you're interested in seeing those places, your request might be granted. Even a quick one-minute peek could give you some insight about working conditions.

And such a quick peek could be enough to make a person think, "I want to be here!" Or it can make a person ask, "Do I really want to be here?" Either way, the more you learn beforehand, the better a position you'll be in to figure out if you would be happy in this line of work.

So You Want to Work on a Boat

# *I Like Being Around Boats but I Think I'll Stay on Shore*

Some people like being around boats, but aren't crazy about leaving behind their land-based lifestyle. There are others who've worked on the water long enough and want to come ashore to enjoy a more stable family life. Whatever the reason for seeking alternatives to shipboard life, there are plenty of options on shore. As with everything else, the more experience, education, and training that someone has, the more attractive the choices can be.

Many maritime companies are happy to snap up former navigation and engine room personnel for shoreside positions in their marine operations departments. But there are good opportunities for jobseekers who've never even worked on the water. These positions arise in shipbuilding, maritime security, yacht sales, customer service, plant operations, marine insurance, and other areas. Payscales can range from minimum wage to six figures, depending on qualifications.

**Port Captain** Port captains handle managerial duties, often for a fleet of vessels. They inspect vessels in port, brief officers on regulatory developments, investigate spills, assist in preparing reports for marine incidents, oversee hiring, and sometimes handle training duties. They may coordinate company-wide programs, such as the implementation of STCW or ECDIS compliance.

Port captains generally have extensive sea time behind them. Some companies use the title **marine operations superintendent** to describe someone who handles these duties. As with port engineers, port captain vacancies don't arise as frequently as seagoing positions. And when openings do arise, people often line up for the chance to come ashore.

**Port Engineer** Port engineers oversee maintenance programs for organizations that generally own a fleet of vessels, such as tugboat, ferry, or fishing vessel operators. They manage oil analysis and other preventive maintenance programs. They coordinate overhauls and major repairs with in-house personnel and vendors. Some companies look for familiarity with certain powertrains, such as Fairbanks Morse, EMD, or Cummins, because their fleets are primarily powered by those engines. But that isn't always the case.

Basic computer, writing, and database skills are needed to handle vendor correspondence and parts inventory spreadsheets. Basic mathematical skills are needed to understand decimals and read micrometers, calipers, and other measurement instruments. Machine shop skills with lathes, mills, drill presses, and shapers are a big asset, as are welding and burning skills.

**Dispatcher** Dispatchers assign jobs to tugboats. They need to understand the logistics of vessels traveling to and from jobs and how much time each job requires. Familiarity with local waters, as well as a working knowledge of tide and current charts, can be helpful in scheduling jobs in a logical and cost-effective manner.

A good dispatcher understands the strengths and weaknesses of all vessels in a fleet, in terms of horsepower, number of screws, special maneuvering attributes, and age limitations. Good communication skills are necessary to ensure that instructions are clearly understood by vessel crews.

**A community service** Some shipyards run apprenticeship programs in which they train local residents to become welders. The programs can be coordinated with local colleges or training institutes, and are sometimes offered at no cost. Such programs enable a company to give something back to the community where they do business, while providing the company with a skilled workforce, made up of home-grown talent. Welding is a fundamental aspect of shipbuilding, and it takes time to develop good welders.

**Customer service** and **ticket reservation positions** regularly arise with cruise ship, ferry, water taxi, tour boat, and dinner cruise operators. The positions require strong interpersonal skills to deal with customers on the telephone, in person, and online. Diplomacy and negotiating skills can also be helpful, as these jobs can require the ability to resolve customer complaints or demands for refunds.

**Shipyards** offer a diverse assortment of positions dealing with vessel construction, repair, or dismantling. With a few exceptions, shipyard jobs generally require a high degree of technical skills. In some regions, there are occasional entry-level opportunities, where shipyards hire apprentice candidates from the local area and train them from the ground up.

Shipyard tradespeople include **welders**, who fuse together steel or aluminum plates, beams, and other components with arc welding equipment. Welding has become a very sophisticated technology, advancing light years beyond the portable machines used by recreational welders to build boat trailers in their backyards. There are MIG, TIG, Plasma Arc, and other welding technologies that need to be learned to work as a welder in a shipyard.

Where you find welders, you'll also find **burners**, who use oxy-acetylene torches to cut through steel. Sometimes, welders handle both tasks. Burners cut openings in bulkheads, remove structures, or dismantle entire vessels for scrap. The latter activity is a specialized field in itself called shipbreaking. Combining the art of the burner with computers, **numerically controlled cutting** uses plasma arc torches to cut structural components from flat panels of steel. The torches are guided by computer programs into which operators enter dimensions for bulkheads, frames, and other components.

**Machinists** operate lathes, milling machines, shapers, drill presses, and other machine tools to fabricate parts. Machinists today use numerically controlled equipment. Like numerically controlled metal cutting, machine tools are guided by computer programs. Machinists enter dimensions into a computer which guides turning, boring, cutting, milling, and drilling operations. The process is more economical than manual methods and can reduce the chances for errors resulting from performing tedious and repetitive machining operations.

**Maritime museums** offer shoreside opportunities for people who tend to be attracted to maritime heritage and history. These museums are usually created by the retirement of famous warships. The work can be fulfilling, but paying positions can be limited. On some museum ships, volunteers carry out many duties, such as restoration, maintenance, and conducting tours for the public. Above, the USS Hornet (CVS-12) takes on either fuel oil or aviation fuel from the USS Sacramento (AOE-1). The photo was taken in June 1967 on the South China Sea during the Vietnam War. The Hornet now serves as a museum in Alameda, California. Other aircraft carriers that serve as museums include USS Midway, in San Diego and USS Intrepid, in New York City.

**Riggers** and **crane operators** use cranes, chain falls, hydraulic jacks, and other equipment to move large components. They may remove a gas turbine from the machinery spaces of a ship, or move a modular sub-assembly for a superstructure across a shipyard. They also align equipment. Although they handle machinery that can weigh several tons, riggers work with tolerances in the order of thousandths of inches.

**Electricians** set up electrical distribution systems and control panels. They run wiring for motors, lights, elevators, and other equipment. They coordinate with riggers for aligning electric motors with pumps, compressors, and blowers. They may work with **instrumentation & control technicians** in setting up control panels.

**Plumbers** set up shipboard piping, including drains, bilge piping, ballast water systems, sinks, showers, and toilets. **Steamfitters** set up and repair piping for high-pressure steam and fluid systems. This can involve precision standards because failure of a pipe carrying 1,200 psi steam can carry disastrous consequences. They may work with mil-specs, short for military specifications, in laying out piping systems aboard naval vessels.

**Carpenters** construct wood structures, such as framing, paneling, doors, and hatches. **Cabinetmakers** also work with wood, but they specialize in furniture quality fixtures. This can include cabinets and countertops in the galley or navigation consoles on the bridge.

**Estimators** review construction projects and determine the cost of labor and materials. It's an important position for a shipyard's bottom line. If an estimator overbids a job, the yard can lose a prospective client. But if an estimator underbids a job, the yard can lose money and be forced to pay overtime or contract penalties.

**Sheet metal fabricators** use presses and cutters to form cabinets, desks, bunks and other structures from sheet metal. They may work with welders or use rivets to joint panels together. **Sandblasters** prepare surfaces for painting by stripping them down to bare metal.

**Painters** apply paints and other specialized coatings to vessel interiors and exteriors. In some cases, they chemically prepare surfaces to be salt-free before expensive coatings are applied. They also apply anti-fouling coatings to underwater surfaces. **Laborers** carry equipment, supplies, and keep work areas clean.

**Shipbuilding jobs** comprise one of the largest sectors of shoreside employment in the maritime industry. Shipyards offer job opportunities for engineers, designers, estimators, welders, machinists, pipefitters, plumbers, electricians, carpenters, painters, sandblasters, and laborers. It's interesting how much shipbuilding has evolved since the days of World War II. This is a far cry from the days when some Liberty Ships were built in the record time of four or five days. Today, large ships can take several years to complete, since they are built to the highest quality standards. However, as the chart above illustrates, the emphasis in ship construction during World War II was on quantity. In the photo above, Victory Ships and Liberty Ships are lined up at California Shipbuilding Corporation.

**Yacht Clubs and Marinas** offer job opportunities in **customer service** and **maintenance**. Launch operators (who were already discussed in an earlier chapter) drive boats, called tenders, which carry guests to and from their yachts. There are also positions for **dockmasters**, who check the membership of guests at the gate. Dockmasters also issue slips to visiting boats and oversee usage of electricity and other utilities.

**Yacht brokerages** offer an opportunity to combine sales skills with boat knowledge. Yacht brokers represent parties in the sale and purchase of recreational vessels. Since boat buyers tend to do a lot of research before entering a deal, successful brokers need to be knowledgeable in many areas, including yacht design, exotic sail materials, diesel fuel problems, and fiberglass repair, just to name a few. Some experienced brokers are equally at ease in discussing PHRF ratings for vintage sailboats, or engine options that were once available on older motor yachts. This can be a difficult line of work because a broker's income is generally based on commission. There are also brokerages that specialize in commercial vessels. Essentially, the same rules about knowing your product apply.

**Maintenance personnel** maintain equipment and recreational areas. In yacht clubs with junior sailing programs, job opportunities arise for **sailing instructors**. Sailing instructors generally need several years of sailing and racing experience, together with certification from a recognized sailing organization.

**Boatyards** offer employment geared around the storage, launching, hauling, and maintenance of pleasure boats. In northern latitudes, the positions can be seasonal in nature. Peak workloads arise in the spring, when boats are launched, and in the fall, when boats are hauled.

**Boat handlers** move boats using travelifts, forklifts, or cranes. It's a somewhat loose title, since boat handlers also perform maintenance, painting, and repairs in small yards where launching and hauling traffic won't keep someone employed on a full-time basis.

Boatyards hire **marine mechanics** to work on diesel engines, gas engines, outdrives, and outboards. Boatyards also hire **general laborers**, **painters**, and **fiberglass technicians**. Fiberglass technicians use fiberglass cloth and resins to repair damaged boats.

Large yards may have an in-house **rigger**, which is different from a rigger in a shipyard. A boatyard rigger deals with sailboat rigging, such as the forestays, shrouds, and backstays that support the mast. Riggers may also splice running rigging, such as halyards and sheets used to raise and trim sails.

**Cargo Operations** positions regularly arise in large shipping companies. These include **freight agents**, who arrange for cargo to travel from one port to another. They prepare bills of lading and other shipping documents. They choose the means by which goods will be picked up, shipped, and delivered. This can require an understanding of intermodal shipping, where goods move from container ship to cargo terminal to rail carrier to road carrier to final destination.

Cargo operations positions also include **cargo terminal supervisors**, who coordinate the loading and offloading of cargo ships, railway cars, and trucks. They are responsible for ensuring the timely movement of goods across various modes of transportation. They supervise **crane operators, longshoremen, warehouse workers**, and other personnel who physically operate the equipment used in moving and storing goods. These jobs can require certification to use cranes, forklifts, and other material handling equipment.

**Marine Insurance** positions include **underwriters, claims representatives, investigators** and **sales agents**. Underwriters prepare policies for clients, who are known as insureds. Preparing a policy requires expertise in identifying the risks to be covered and setting reasonable policy limits. **Sales agents** sell insurance to clients, based on their needs and budgets. Sales agents generally coordinate with underwriters to develop policies. **Claim representatives** handle property and casualty claims for losses involving personal injury, hull damage, machinery damage, or cargo damage.

In a property loss matter, claim representatives review surveyor reports and bills of lading. They sometimes go to the field to personally inspect damage, and then prepare recommendations as to whether a claim should be paid. They must possess strong negotiation skills because the figure they propose to settle a matter can be less than the amount demanded by a claimant. If negotiations aren't fruitful, the claimant may sue. In those instances, claims representatives arrange for attorneys to defend claims.

**Investigators** closely examine property and casualty losses. Investigators are not usually called in on every claim. Generally, if something seems questionable, an insurance company will arrange a special investigation. For instance, if an employee files an injury claim that the insurance company finds suspicious, an investigator may be sent to follow him around to determine the validity of a disability or injury.

**Unlike shipboard marine engineers** who usually work four on and eight off, shoreside stationary engineers generally work eight or twelve-hour days. One typical scheduling scheme consists of a week of 7 to 3 watches, a week of 3 to 11 watches, a week of 11 to 7 watches, and a week of day work as *idler* or *floater*, squeezed in every several weeks. Being an idler or floater means a person goes to work, but isn't on watch. This is to provide periodic windows to allow for training, testing, or taking vacation days. Such a schedule is called a rotating shift and is common in large base load electric generating stations. In schools and smaller institutions, the job of a stationary engineer could be a day job.

**Maritime Museums** may seem a little off the beaten path. Museums are often centered around historic ships that have been retired. They can offer employment opportunities as **tour guides**, **security guards**, **maintenance workers**, **ticket sales agents**, **fundraising specialists**, and **marketing specialists**. Some of the positions are ideal for people who enjoy maritime history and who have an interest in the technical aspects of ships. Since these positions involve interaction with the public, good interpersonal skills are necessary. Because museums generally operate on grants and charitable donations, their budgets can be limited, resulting in some of these positions being filled by volunteers.

**Maritime Education and Training** are important sectors of this job market. Opportunities arise on many different levels at maritime academies, colleges, vocational schools, training institutes, and specialized high schools. Required areas of expertise include shipboard operations, navigation, seamanship, engineering, and other maritime subjects.

Qualifications for the training and education sector can be diverse. **Professors** and **instructors** for operations-oriented courses at maritime academies generally hold college degrees and Coast Guard licenses. They usually have extensive shipboard experience and can be assisted by **non-licensed deck and engine personnel** on school training ships and in marine operations labs.

Some commercial mariners teach Coast Guard license prep courses in a training institute setting without holding a college degree. In those instances, the key job requirement is generally holding a certain grade of license. There are also vocational schools and specialty high schools that focus on providing students with an introduction to the maritime industry. In these institutions, **teachers** are usually required to hold state teaching licenses.

**Plant Operations** A **stationary engineer** is someone who operates a steam or electric plant in a shoreside facility. Technically, this is not part of the maritime industry. But it's about as close as one can get to working in an engine room without going to sea. Openings generally arise in electric utilities, hospitals, and schools. In large utilities that operate fossil-fired plants, stationary engineers, sometimes called shift supervisors, are assisted by **power**

**plant mechanics** and **control board operators**. The stationary engineer is comparable to an engineering officer on a ship, while mechanics are comparable to oilers or other QMEDs. Stationary engineers must generally take an examination to operate high-pressure boilers.

**Marine Surveying** is a technical area that generally requires a background in marine engineering, naval architecture, electrical engineering, or ocean engineering. Surveyors are employed by classification societies, which are organizations that inspect vessels and offshore structures for compliance with structural, machinery, piping, and electrical codes.

Employers include the American Bureau of Shipping, Germanischer Lloyd, and Bureau Veritas. There are other types of marine surveyors, such as those hired by yacht buyers who want an inspection report. Those types of surveys are performed to determine the condition of a yacht and are generally required by insurance companies before issuing a policy.

**Maritime Security** has become a very prominent sector of the industry since September 11, 2001. Ships, cargo terminals, and passenger terminals have become the focus of measures aimed at protecting national security. Job opportunities arise with government agencies, port authorities, and private security contractors.

Positions range from entry-level **security guards** to experienced **security superintendents** for large port facilities. **Cargo inspectors** have become a focal point in checking containers for the entry of explosives, radioactive materials, biological agents, and other hazardous threats. They use radiography and other techniques to examine the contents of containers and packages.

Many of the jobseekers in this area have military or law enforcement backgrounds, which includes small arms training. Maritime security specialists sometimes work jointly with marine inspection personnel.

**Maritime security will continue** to see the use of sophisticated technologies. In the photo above, U.S. Customs Service and U.S. Coast Guard personnel work together in a multi-agency task force operation in Houston, Texas. They are using a VACIS, which stands for Vehicle and Cargo Inspection System. It uses gamma-ray imaging to examine cargo shipments. The SAIC* system enables operators to see the contents of closed containers through more than 6" of steel. 70 *Science Applications International Corporation

Marine inspection is closely related to maritime security activities. Typical backgrounds include experience in vessel operations, as in the case of **inspectors** who board ships entering ports. They examine logbooks and other shipboard documents.

Ideal candidates are former officers who have an appreciation of issues involving oily water separators, ballast water management, marine sanitation, and air emissions. In addition to having insight into shipboard operations, inspectors need to be familiar with classification society, Coast Guard, and local environmental regulations.

**Fisheries Industries** With increasingly strict regulations governing catch sizes and the quantity of fish caught, many jobseekers have sought alternatives to working on commercial fishing vessels. One such alternative has been the aquaculture industry. Positions in this field can range from **biologists**, who hold advanced degrees, to **technicians** and **mechanics** who oversee the operation and maintenance of floatation systems, netting, water circulation systems, and other equipment.

**Canal lock operators** work on inland waterways and facilitate vessel traffic through canal locks. They operate gates, raise and lower water levels, and direct vessels in entering and leaving locks. In addition to operations, canal systems hire **maintenance mechanics** to repair and maintain equipment such as gates, pumps, motors, valves, and piping systems.

There are many additional opportunities in maritime companies that aren't discussed here. These include purchasing agents, website designers, communications specialists, computer programmers, and administrative assistants, among others. These positions are really outside the scope of this book.

However, it's something to keep in mind that shipyards, diesel engine manufacturers, marine insurance companies, and other maritime industry employers tend to have a wide array of general employment opportunities beyond the traditional marine-based options discussed in this chapter. The larger the organization, the more diverse the range of opportunities.

## Vessel Operator Lists

The following pages contain lists of companies that operate commercial vessels, or that may ship cargo through chartered vessels or subsidiaries. These lists are provided as reference only. The fact that a company is listed here does not necessarily mean that it is hiring or recruiting, or that it is even interested in unsolicited employment inquiries. However, many of the companies listed below and in the next several pages do have employment sections in their websites. Those employment sections can be a good place to start a job search.

## Ocean-Going Vessel Operators

Some of these companies may fill their shipboard positions through maritime unions and recruitment agencies. However, even when they do not post shipboard openings, many companies generally provide information or links that steer jobseekers in the right direction.

APL
Atlantic Container Line
BP
CMA-CGM
ConocoPhillips - Polar Tankers
Dockwise
Evergreen Line
ExxonMobil
Hapag-Lloyd
Hess
Höegh
Horizon Lines
I.M. Skaugen
K Line
Maersk
Matson

Mediterranean Shipping Company
NYK Line
Oldendorff Carriers
OSG - Overseas Shipholding Group
P&O Nedllyod
Seabulk Shipping
Shell
Stolt Tankers
Teekay Tankers
Texaco
Wallenius Wilhelmsen Logistics

## Cruise Lines

American Cruise Lines
Bora Bora Cruises
Carnival Cruise Lines
Celebrity Cruises
Costa Cruises
Crystal Cruises
Cunard Cruise Line
Disney Cruise Line
Holland America Line
Norwegian Cruise Line
P&O Cruises
Premier Cruise Line
Princess Cruises
Regent Seven Seas Cruises
Royal Caribbean International
Seabourn Cruise Line
Silversea Cruises
Star Clippers
Windstar Cruise Line

## Tugboat, Towing, and Oil & Gas Industry Vessel Operators

This list includes operators of OSVs, PSVs, AHTs, and utility vessels. The geographic range in this list is far-reaching, with some of the companies operating internationally, and others operating strictly on inland rivers. Included in the group are companies that handle marine construction.

American Electric Power
American Commercial Lines
Andrie
Bisso Marine
Blessey Marine Services
Bouchard Transportation Co.
Bourbon
Boyer Towing
Brusco Tug and Barge
Catalina Freight Line
Cheramie Marine
Consol Energy
Crosby Tugs
Crounse Corporation
Crowley Maritime Corporation
D & L Salvage
Devall Towing & Boat Service
Donjon Marine Co.
Edison Chouest Offshore
Express Marine
Farstad Shipping
Foss Maritime
The Great Lakes Group
Harley Marine Services

Higman Marine Services

Hodder Tugboat Co.

Hornbeck Offshore Services

Houston Marine Services

Ingram Marine Group

Inland Marine Service

Kirby Corporation

L & M Botruc Rental

Magnolia Marine

Marquette Transportation

McAllister Towing & Transportation

Moran Towing Corporation

Odyssea Marine

Ohio Valley Marine Service

Penn Maritime

Reinauer Transportation

Resolve Marine Group

Sause Bros.

SCF Liquids

Seabulk Towing

Settoon Towing

Stevens Towing

TECO Barge Line

Tidewater Marine

United Maritime Group

The Vane Brothers Company

Warrior & Gulf Navigation

Western Towboat Co.

## Ferry Operators & Water Taxi Operators

Alameda Harbor Bay Ferry

Alaska Marine Highway System

Anderson Ferry

Block Island Ferry

Blue & Gold Fleet

The Bridgeport & Port Jefferson Steamboat Company

Chicago Water Taxi

Cross Sound Ferry

Delaware River and Bay Authority

Hy-Line Cruises

Lake Champlain Ferries

Lake Express

New York Water Taxi

New York Waterway

S.S. Badger - Lake Michigan Car Ferry

Staten Island Ferry (New York City Department of Transportation)

Washington State Ferries (Washington State Department of Transportation)

## Research Vessel Operators

Research vessels are operated privately and by the government. The National Oceanic and Atmospheric Administration, or NOAA, operates the largest fleet of research vessels in the United States. NOAA posts job vacancies on the federal employment website, www.usajobs.gov. Other research vessel operators are listed below:

Duke/University of North Carolina Oceanographic Consortium

Florida Institute of Oceanography

Lamont-Doherty Earth Observatory

Monterey Bay Aquarium Research Institute

National Science Foundation

Scripps Institution of Oceanography

Skidaway Institute of Oceanography

United States Antarctic Program

Woods Hole Oceanographic Institution

## Dinner Cruise Vessel Operators

Hornblower Cruises and Events
San Diego Tours
Seattle Tours
Spirit Cruises
SpiritLine Cruises
Starfleet Yachts
StarLite Cruises
World Yacht

## Tour, Excursion, and Sightseeing Vessel Operators

Argosy Cruises
Arkansas Queen Riverboat
BB Riverboats
Boston Harbor Cruises
Capital Cruises
Chattanooga Tours
Circle Line Downtown
Circle Line Sightseeing Cruises
Fort Lauderdale Sightseeing Cruises
Island Queen Cruises
Old Forge Lake Cruises
Padelford Riverboats
Potomac Riverboat Company
Red & White Fleet
Shoreline Sightseeing Cruises
Spirit of Peoria
Wendella Boat Tours

## Marine Construction & Dredging Companies

Apollo Environmental Strategies

Cashman Dredging

Cottrell Contracting Corporation

Dredge America

Great Lakes Dredge & Dock Company

Manson Construction Company

Marinex Construction

Orion Marine Group

Southern Dredging Company

Vortex Marine Construction

Weeks Marine


The U.S. Army Corps of Engineers - This is a federal agency that handles dredging projects.

## Additional Sample License Questions

These are additional sample questions of the type that have appeared on license exams. These questions are NOT endorsed by the U.S.C.G. as license exam questions.

### Sample License Questions - General Deck

---

1. You are scheduled to load a bulk shipment of steel turnings. Which statement is TRUE?

(a.) The primary hazard of this cargo is that it is subject to spontaneous heating and ignition.

(b.) The shipping papers should describe this cargo as "Waste; steel borings."

(c.) After loading, you may not sail if the temperature in each hold of steel turnings exceeds 130° F.

(d.) This cargo may not be transported in bulk unless a special permit is issued by the Coast Guard.

---

2. A vessel is entering port and has a pilot conning the vessel. The master is unsure that the pilot is taking sufficient action to prevent a collision. What should the master do?

(a.) Nothing; the pilot is required by law and is solely responsible for the safety of the vessel.

(b.) State his concerns to the pilot but do not interfere with the handling of the vessel.

(c.) Recommend an alternative action and if not followed relieve the pilot.

(d.) Direct the pilot to stop the vessel and anchor if necessary until the situation clears.

---

3. You are in charge of a U.S. documented vessel. Under title 46 of the United States Code, if you fail to report a complaint of a sexual offense, you may be _____.

(a.) held personally liable by the victim and sued

(b.) criminally charged and jailed

(c.) civilly charged and fined

(d.) All of the above are correct

---

4. Which statement about damage control is TRUE?

(a.) A hole in the hull at the waterline is more dangerous than a hole below the inner bottom.

(b.) The amount of water entering a ship through a hole varies inversely to the area of the hole.

(c.) Water flowing into a lower compartment on a ship is more dangerous than water on deck or flowing into an upper compartment.

(d.) Water flowing over the fo'c'sle bulwark is more dangerous than a hole in the hull at the waterline.

5. You are going ahead on twin engines with rudder amidships. Your starboard engine stalls. To continue on course, you should _____.

(a.) apply left rudder

(b.) apply right rudder

(c.) increase engine speed

(d.) keep your rudder amidships

6. Bilge soundings indicate _____.

(a.) the amount of condensation in the hold

(b.) whether the cargo is leaking or not

(c.) whether the vessel is taking on water

(d.) All of the above

Answers to General Deck Questions 1- 6

(1.) a  (2.) c  (3.) c  (4.) a  (5.) a  (6.) d

## Sample License Questions - General Engine

1. A portion of the cargo of an LNG carrier boils off during each voyage. How is the cargo boil off normally handled?

(a.) compressed, condensed, and returned to the cargo tanks

(b.) vented to the atmosphere

(c.) burned in the boilers

(d.) mixed with nitrogen and recirculated through the primary barrier

---

2. In accordance with Coast Guard Regulations (46 CFR), which of the following situations requires an official logbook entry and is considered the responsibility of the chief engineer?

(a.) ensuring that the emergency lighting and power systems are operated and inspected at least once in each week the vessel is navigated

(b.) seeing that all lifeboat winch control apparatus, including motor controllers, limit switches, etc. are examined at least once in each 3 months

(c.) obtaining a sample of all fuel oil received on board to be used as fuel along with ascertaining all particulars such as vendor, producer, flash point, etc.

(d.) All of the above

---

3. The letters 'NC' in '1/4-20 NC' indicate the bolt is _____.

(a.) made of nickel cadmium metal

(b.) made of non-corrosive metal

(c.) not clad with any coating

(d.) threaded with national coarse threads

---

4. A cofferdam is a/an _____.

(a.) empty space between tank tops and bilges

(b.) cement baffle in a fresh water tank

(c.) tank for storing chemicals

(d.) empty space separating compartments to prevent the contents of one compartment from entering another in case of leakage

5. A lube oil filter can be used to remove most contaminants from lube oil. A contaminant which will remain in the lube oil after filtering is _____.

(a.) acid

(b.) diesel oil

(c.) sediment

(d.) water

---

6. On small passenger vessels of less than 100 gross tons, watertight doors and watertight hatches are _____.

(a.) not required to be marked

(b.) required to be marked, but on only one side

(c.) require to be marked on both sides in clearly legible letters at least 25 millimeters ( 1 inch) high

(d.) none of the above

---

Answers to General Engine Questions 1- 6

(1.) c   (2.) c   (3.) d   (4.) d   (5.) b   (6.) c

**Sample License Questions - General Navigation**

---

1. An anemometer on a moving vessel measures _____.

(a.) apparent wind speed only

(b.) true wind speed and true wind direction

(c.) true wind speed

(d.) apparent wind speed and true wind

---

2. In the celestial equator system of coordinates, what is comparable to latitude on the terrestrial sphere?

(a.) altitude

(b.) right ascension

(c.) celestial meridians

(d.) declination

---

3. Magnetic compass deviation _____.

(a.) varies, depending upon the bearing used

(b.) is the angular difference between magnetic north and compass north

(c.) is published on the compass rose on most nautical charts

(d.) is the angular difference between geographic and magnetic meridians

---

4. You have another ship overtaking you close aboard to starboard. You have 3 radar targets bearing 090° relative at ranges of .5 mile, 1 mile, and 1.5 miles. In this case, the unwanted echoes are called _____.

(a.) multiple echoes

(b.) spoking

(c.) indirect echoes

(d.) side-lobe echoes

---

5. Which statement concerning the operation of radar in fog is TRUE?

(a.) Radar ranges are less accurate in fog.

(b.) Navigation buoys will always show up on radar.

(c.) A sandy beach will show up clearer on radar than a rocky cliff.

(d.) Small wooden boats may not show up on radar.

6. You are approaching Chatham Strait from the south in foggy weather. You have Coronation Island and Hazy Islands on the radar. Suddenly the radar malfunctions. You then resort to using whistle echoes to determine your distance off Coronation Island. Your stopwatch reads 16.3 seconds for the echo to be heard. How far are you off Coronation Island?

(a.) 1.0 mile

(b.) 1.5 miles

(c.) 2.0 miles

(d.) 2.5 miles

Answers to General Navigation Questions 1- 6

(1.) a  (2.) d  (3.) b  (4.) a  (5.) d  (6.) b

**Sample License Questions - Engineering Safety**

1. The most frequent incidents of tanker pollution occurring during tanker operations is _____.

(a.) due to collisions

(b.) routine discharge of oil during ballasting and tank crude oil washing

(c.) loading and discharging

(d.) due solely to groundings

2. Why is it important for fuel oil tanks not to be topped off when loading cold oil?

(a.) Increased viscosity of the product needs higher loading pressure, which increases the chance of a spill.

(b.) Air pockets may cause the fuel to bubble out of the ullage hole.

(c.) The change in its specific volume when heated may cause an overflow.

(d.) The fueling valve may become stuck closed and cause the fuel oil to spill before the valve can be opened.

3. To be in compliance with U.S. Federal Ballast Water Management regulations, which of the following procedures may be followed by an ocean vessel entering U.S. waters returning from an international voyage?

(a.) Prior to discharging ballast water in U.S. waters, the vessel must perform a complete ballast water exchange in an area no less than 100 nautical miles from any shoreline.

(b.) Ballast water may only be discharged overboard if the vessel is underway.

(c.) Prior to entering U.S. waters, a vessel may use any Coast Guard approved alternative environmentally sound method of BWM.

(d.) Ballast water may only be discharged overboard through an approved oily water separator.

4. An oil fire would be classified as a _____.

(a.) class A

(b.) class B

(c.) class C

(d.) class D

5. If you have to jump in the water when abandoning ship, your legs should be
_____.

(a.) spread apart as far as possible

(b.) held as tightly against your chest as possible

(c.) in a kneeling position

(d.) extended straight down and crossed at the ankles

Answers to Engineering Safety Questions 1- 5

(1.) c    (2.) c    (3.) c    (4.) b    (5.) d

**Sample License Questions - Collision Regs**

---

1. BOTH INTERNATIONAL & INLAND Traffic Separation Schemes established by the International Maritime Organization _____.

(a.) provide inbound and outbound lanes to promote the safe flow of vessel traffic

(b.) provide vessel reporting systems to assist in search and rescue in the event of a vessel casualty

(c.) provide routing and vessel scheduling procedures to reduce shipping delays

(d.) prohibit vessels carrying hazardous cargos from entering waters that are environmentally sensitive

---

2. BOTH INTERNATIONAL & INLAND In a crossing situation, a vessel fishing must keep out of the way of a vessel which is _____.

(a.) under sail

(b.) towing

(c.) restricted in her ability to maneuver

(d.) engaged in pilotage duty

---

3. INTERNATIONAL ONLY Which vessel shall avoid impeding the safe passage of a vessel constrained by her draft?

(a.) a vessel not under command

(b.) a sailing vessel

(c.) a vessel restricted in her ability to maneuver

(d.) all of the above

---

4. BOTH INTERNATIONAL & INLAND A head-on situation at night is one in which you see _____.

(a.) one sidelight of a vessel ahead of you

(b.) one sidelight and a masthead light of a vessel ahead of you

(c.) one sidelight, a masthead light, and a range light of a vessel ahead of you

(d.) both sidelights of a vessel dead ahead of you

---

5. INLAND ONLY What is the required whistle signal for a power-driven vessel leaving a dock or berth?

(a.) One short blast

(b.) One prolonged blast

(c.) Two short blasts

(d.) Two prolonged blasts

6. INLAND ONLY A vessel displaying a flashing blue light is _____.

(a.) transferring dangerous cargo

(b.) a law enforcement vessel

(c.) a work boat

(d.) engaged in a race

Answers to Collision Regs Questions 1- 7

(1.) a  (2.) c  (3.) b  (4.) d  (5.) b  (6.) b

## Sample License Questions - Steam Plants

---

1. Boiler firesides must be kept free of soot accumulations because _____.

(a.) soot interferes with the flow of feedwater

(b.) the steam drum internals will become clogged

(c.) the fuel oil heaters will become overloaded

(d.) soot insulates the boiler heating surfaces

---

2. To stop the rotor of a main turbine while underway at sea you should _____.

(a.) apply the prony brake

(b.) tighten the stern tube packing gland

(c.) secure all steam to the turbine

(d.) admit astern steam to the turbine after securing the ahead steam

---

3. Gland sealing steam is used during steam turbine operation to prevent the loss of _____.

(a.) oil

(b.) air

(c.) vacuum

(d.) temperature

---

4. Concerning the classification of steam turbines, a cross compound designed unit _____.

(a.) consists of reaction stages and a dummy piston

(b.) consists of one Curtis stage and reaction blading

(c.) consists of a high pressure turbine, crossover pipe, and low pressure turbine

(d.) is made up of a varied assortment of impulse and reaction staging

---

5. If the main and standby lube oil service pumps of the main engine fail while underway at sea, _____.

(a.) an emergency supply of oil in the gravity tank will provide time to crash stop the turbine and gears

(b.) the reduction gear bearings will immediately fail

(c.) the turbine bearings will immediately fail

(d.) emergency lubrication can be supplied through the use of the hand pump

6. Boiler tube failures can result from _____.

(a.) corrosion

(b.) overheating

(c.) mechanical stress

(d.) all of the above

Answers to Steam Plant Questions 1- 6

(1.) d  (2.) d  (3.) c  (4.) c  (5.) a  (6.) d

## Sample License Questions - General Safety (Deck)

---

1. All of the following are part of the fire triangle EXCEPT _____.

(a.) electricity

(b.) fuel

(c.) oxygen

(d.) heat

---

2. On a survival craft, VHF radio precautions shall be taken to prevent the inadvertent selection of which channel ?

(a.) 6

(b.) 8

(c.) 16

(d.) 22

---

3. An inert gas system installed on a tanker is designed to _____.

(a.) aid in the stripping and cleaning of cargo tanks

(b.) increase the rate of discharge of cargo

(c.) force toxic and explosive fumes from a cargo tank to vent to the outside atmosphere

(d.) lower the oxygen levels inside cargo tanks, making explosion nearly impossible

---

4. An airplane wants a vessel to change course and proceed towards another vessel in distress. The actions of the aircraft to convey this message will NOT include _____.

(a.) circling the vessel at least once

(b.) heading in the direction of the distress location

(c.) flashing the navigation lights on and off

(d.) crossing ahead and rocking the wings

---

5. Your ship is returning to New Orleans from a foreign voyage and carrying a bulk cargo of anhydrous ammonia. You must notify the Captain of the Port, New Orleans, _____.

(a.) at least 96 hours before entering port

(b.) if you are not participating in the USMER system

(c.) only if you have a hazardous condition aboard

(d.) only if your arrival will vary more than six hours from your ETA reported to AMVER

6. Your vessel is broken down and rolling in heavy seas. You can reduce the possibility of capsizing by _____.

(a.) moving all personnel aft

(b.) constantly shifting the rudder

(c.) rigging a sea anchor

(d.) moving all personnel forward and low

7. When lifting loads from a boat in heavy weather, the load should be taken when the boat _____.

(a.) reaches the crest

(b.) begins to fall

(c.) begins to rise

(d.) reaches the trough

Answers to General Safety (Deck) Questions 1- 7

(1.) a  (2.) c  (3.) d  (4.) c  (5.) a  (6.) c  (7.) a

## Sample License Questions - Electricity

1. On a vessel with turbo-electric drive, which of the following conditions would indicate that the propulsion motor had dropped out of synchronization with the propulsion generator?

(a.) Excessive vibration of the vessel

(b.) Tripped main motor interlocks

(c.) Overheated crosstie busses

(d.) Closed contact in the field circuits

2. A circuit breaker and a fuse have a basic similarity in that they both _____.

(a.) can be reset to energize the circuit

(b.) should open the circuit when overloaded

(c.) will burn out when an over current flow develops

(d.) all of the above

3. Transformers are used onboard ships with AC generators to _____.

(a.) change line frequency value

(b.) increase power output to modulating frequency controllers

(c.) decrease power output to modulating frequency controllers

(d.) provide different voltage values to operate various types of electrical equipment

4. The electrolyte in a lead-acid storage battery consists of distilled water and _____.

(a.) hydrogen chloride

(b.) calcium chloride

(c.) sulfuric acid

(d.) muriatic acid

5. Which of the electrical properties listed will always be the same across each component in a parallel circuit?

(a.) impedance

(b.) current

(c.) resistance

(d.) voltage

6. The speed of a multi-speed, squirrel-cage, induction motor operating in a fixed frequency system can be changed by _____.

(a.) reconnecting stator windings for different numbers of poles

(b.) changing the RPM of the rotor flux

(c.) changing the phase sequence of the applied voltage

(d.) reconnecting the stator so that no poles have the same polarity

7. While standing an "at sea watch" onboard a DC diesel-electric drive ship, you notice the transformer core temperature slowly rising. You should first _____.

(a.) check the transformer ventilation fans for proper operation

(b.) notify the bridge that you need to slow down

(c.) send the oiler to look for fires in the transformer

(d.) reduce load by tripping lighting circuits

Answers to Electricity Questions 1- 7

(1.) a  (2.) b  (3.) d  (4.) c  (5.) d  (6.) a  (7.) a

## Sample License Questions - Motor Plants & Auxiliaries

1. How is the concentration of dissolved oxygen in the feedwater of an auxiliary boiler maintained at acceptable limits?

(a.) Feedwater is cycled through a DC heater.

(b.) Feedwater is treated with phosphates.

(c.) Oxygen is liberated in the three-stages of feedwater preheating.

(d.) Oxygen is liberated by maintaining the highest practical feedwater temperature.

---

2. The most common cause of scale formation in an auxiliary boiler is _____.

(a.) concentrations of calcium sulfate in the boiler water

(b.) fuel oil in the feedwater

(c.) improper treatment of the feedwater with calcium sulfate

(d.) excessive feedwater alkalinity

---

3. A cracked cylinder head on a diesel engine may be indicated by _____.

(a.) excessive lube oil consumption

(b.) water draining from the fuel leak off valves

(c.) combustion gases venting at the expansion tank

(d.) excessive fuel oil consumption

---

4. Low compression in a diesel engine can be caused by _____.

(a.) clogged coolant passages

(b.) a leaking cylinder head gasket

(c.) low fuel oil pressure

(d.) worn or broken cylinder liner sealing rings

---

5. A supercharged diesel engine, when compared to a similar naturally aspirated diesel engine, will develop an increase in _____.

(a.) ignition lag

(b.) engine horsepower

(c.) lube oil system pressure

(d.) specific fuel consumption

6. A large, low-speed, main propulsion diesel engine uses sea water to directly cool the _____.

(a.) cylinder heads

(b.) exhaust valves

(c.) scavenging air

(d.) injectors

---

7. In comparison to exhaust valves, intake valves of diesel engines may be fabricated from low-alloy steels because _____.

(a.) the beveled edges of the intake valves provide for self-centering during seating

(b.) intake valves utilize stellite-coated valve seat inserts which reduce wear

(c.) the effective volume of air passing through intake valves is less than the effective volume of air passing through exhaust valves

(d.) intake valves are less affected by the corrosive action of exhaust gases

---

Answers to Motor Plants and Auxiliaries Questions 1- 7

(1.) d  (2.) a  (3.) c  (4.) b  (5.) b (6.) c  (7.) d

# References

1. Washington State Department of Transportation

2. U.S. Department of Justice - United States Attorney - District of Alaska - August 22, 2007 Operator of the M/V Selendang Ayu Pleads Guilty to Charges Arising from Grounding in the Aleutians

3. Tulane Maritime Law Journal Summer, 2010; 34 Tul. Mar. L. J. 619 - The Ninth Circuit Breathes Life into a Vessel as a Himalaya Beneficiary: Mazda Motors of America, Inc. v. M/V Cougar Ace, by Gillian Gurley

4. A Night to Remember, by Walter Lord; Holt Rinehart and Winston © 1955, 1976 p. 80

5. Ibid p. 81

6. Ibid p. 83

7. Titanic (1997 movie) from www.imdb.com

8. Sample license questions - U.S.C.G.

9. U.S. Army Corps of Engineers

10. Vessel specifications from www.hapaglloyd.com

11. Vessel specifications from Eidesvik Offshore

12. Vessel specifications from N.O.A.A.

13. U.S. Military Sealift Command

14. U.S. Army Corps of Engineers

15. www.superyachttimes.com

16. www.superyachts.com

17. Reuters - U.S. Cruise Ship Pays Record to Cross Panama Canal, Andrew Beatty, June 11, 2008

18. http://canalmuseum.com

19. Disney Cruise Line

20. Edison Chouest Offshore

21. www.tugboatinformation.com

22. Moran Towing Corporation

23. www.tugboatinformation.com; Captain Eric Takakjian, Harold Tartell

24. www.uboataces.com

25. Excerpt from THE GALAPAGOS TORTOISES, IN THEIR RELATION TO THE WHALING INDUSTRY, BY CHARLES HASKINS TOWNSEND, Director of the New York Aquarium NEW YORK AQUARIUM NATURE SERIES, published by the NEW YORK ZOOLOGICAL SOCIETY, New York, N.Y.

26. www.walleniuslines.com

27. Centers for Disease Control and Prevention

28. Sea Fever, by John Masefield

29. Transportation Safety Administration

30. U.S. Coast Guard

31. Transportation Safety Administration

32. Transportation Safety Administration

33. U.S. Coast Guard

34. Transportation Safety Administration

35. U.S. Military Sealift Command

36. U.S. Military Sealift Command

37. U.S. Coast Guard

38. Department of the Navy - Office of the Chief of Naval Operations - Judge Advocate General Investigation to Inquire into the Circumstances Surrounding the Collision between USS John F. Kennedy (CV 67) and USS Belknap (CG 26) which occurred on 22 November 1975.

39. www.tugboatinformation.com

40. www.hoeghlng.com

41. CNN.com, Nuclear Sub 'Collides' with Tanker, November 15, 2002 - no author listed

42. Navy Cadets Won't Discard Their Sextants
By David W. Chen, New York Times, May 29, 1998

43. United States Merchant Marine Academy

44. U.S. Coast Guard

45. Calhoun MEBA Engineering School

46. California Maritime Academy

47. Fletcher Technical Community College

48. Great Lakes Maritime Academy

49. Kingsborough Community College - Maritime Technology Program

50. Maine Maritime Academy

51. Maritime Institute of Technology and Graduate Studies: Pacific Maritime Institute MITAGS:PMI

52. Massachusetts Maritime Academy

53. Mountwest Community and Technical College

54. Paul Hall Center for Maritime Training and Education

55. Seamen's Church Institute

56. Seattle Maritime Academy

57. Star Center

58. SUNY Maritime College

59. Texas A & M University at Galveston

60. United States Merchant Marine Academy

61. A Night to Remember, by Walter Lord; Holt Rinehart and Winston © 1955, 1976 p. 202

62. Oceanic Steam Navigation Co. v. Mellor, 233 U.S. 718 (1914)

63. Chandris v. Latsis, 515 U.S. 347, 368 (1995)

64. U.S. Department of Justice - United States Attorney - District of Alaska - August 22, 2007 Operator of the M/V Selendang Ayu Pleads Guilty to Charges Arising from Grounding in the Aleutians

65. In the Matter of: Oil Spill by the Amoco Cadiz off the Coast of France on March 16, 1978. United States Court of Appeals for the Seventh Circuit, 954 F.2d 1279

66. United States Coast Guard - Investigation into the Circumstances Surrounding the Sinking of the Uninspected Fishing Vessel Arctic Rose - December 19, 2003

67. www.ship-technology.com

68. USCG Maritime Information eXchange - Port State Information eXchange - T1 Oceania

69. U.S. Coast Guard - 5th District Public Affairs, Coast Guard, NRP focus on mariner safety in upper Chesapeake Bay, November 5, 2010

70. SAIC - Science Applications International Corporation

## Photo Credits

| | |
|---|---|
| Front Cover | copyright Michael Klenetsky |
| Back Cover | photo credit Rydia |
| Dedication | dedication page - U.S.C.G. photo |
| iii | top - copyright Denise Kappa |
| iii | bottom - copyright Luis Vasconcelos |
| iv | top - U.S. Naval Historical Center Photo, photographed by Paul Thompson |
| iv | bottom - U.S. Naval Historical Center Photo |
| p. 2 | copyright Eric Gevaert |
| p. 4 | photo credit Xtrememachineuk |
| p. 6 | copyright Neonriver |
| p. 7 | photo credit Wdobner |
| p. 9 | copyright Darryl Brooks |
| p. 10 | photo credit to author/photographer named Self |
| p. 12 | U.S.C.G. - Unified Command photo |
| p. 13 | U.S. Fish & Wildlife Service - Kevin Bell |
| p. 15 | U.S. Army Corps of Engineers |
| p. 20 | photo credit Le.Ti.Gun |
| p. 22 | U.S. Navy photo - Ray F. Longaker, Jr. |
| p. 23 | photo credit Alasdair McLellan |
| p. 24 | copyright Peter Mautsch |
| p. 26 | N.O.A.A. photo |
| p. 30 | U.S. Air Force photo - Senior Airman Bryan Nealy |
| p. 32 | photo credit VerTego |
| p. 35 | copyright Ingmar Zahorsky |
| p. 40 | copyright Richard Gunion |
| p. 42 | U.S. Navy photo - Mass Communication Specialist 1st Class Krishna Jackson |
| p. 44 | U.S. Navy photo - Mass Communication Specialist 1st Class Davis Anderson |
| p. 45 | copyright Krzysztof Korolonek |

| | |
|---|---|
| p. 48 | U.S.C.G. photo - Petty Officer 3rd Class Erik Swanson |
| p. 49 | IWM Collections Online |
| p. 56 | photo credit - source Bo Randstedt, author Danica |
| p. 59 | U.S. Navy photo |
| p. 61 | U.S.C.G. photo |
| p. 64 | copyright Roza |
| p. 68 | copyright Maxexphoto |
| p. 75 | U.S.C.G. photo - PA2 Mike Hvozda |
| p. 76 | copyright Anysunnyday |
| p. 78 | U.S. Navy photo - Mass Communication Specialist 2nd Class Dominique Pineiro |
| p. 80 | U.S. Navy photo |
| p. 81 | copyright Daniël Leppens |
| p. 82 | upper - copyright Joy Prescott |
| p. 82 | lower - U.S.C.G. photo - Gary Chalker BMC |
| p. 83 | upper - U.S. Navy photo |
| p. 83 | lower - photo credit Thewellman |
| p. 84 | copyright Mayonaise |
| p. 85 | N.O.A.A. photo |
| p. 87 | copyright Eric Gevaert |
| p. 88 | upper - copyright Paula Fisher |
| p. 88 | lower - copyright Hubert Coia |
| p. 90 | copyright Pete Setrac |
| p. 95 | copyright Tom Dowd |
| p. 96 | U.S. Navy photo - Petty Officer 2nd Class Steven King |
| p. 99 | U.S. Navy photo - Chief Journalist Alan J. Baribeau |
| p. 106 | copyright Photoinsel |
| p. 108 | U.S.C.G. photo - PA3 Donnie Brzuska |
| p. 124 | U.S. Navy photo |
| p. 125 | copyright Bernard Maurin |
| p. 126 | U.S.C.G. photo - PA2 Luke Pinneo |

**Disclaimer**

The information in this book is provided as general information only. Laws, regulations, statutes, court decisions, and other information are not provided as legal reference materials. Readers are cautioned to verify the content, completeness, accuracy, and current disposition of any laws, regulations, statutes, or court decisions covered in this book. Readers are advised to consult with a competent attorney for questions they may have about legal issues covered in this book. Sample merchant marine officer license questions in this book may have appeared in previous license examinations. However, they are not endorsed by the U.S. Coast Guard as license exam questions.

So You Want to Work on a Boat

www.ingramcontent.com/pod-product-compliance
Lightning Source LLC
Chambersburg PA
CBHW051451170526
45166CB00001B/196